STRAIGHT
OUTTA
CME

BOBBY JACKSON'S JOURNEY TO THE NFL

STRAIGHT OUTTA CME

BOBBY JACKSON'S JOURNEY TO THE NFL

BILL LIGHTLE

STRAIGHT OUTTA CME
BOBBY JACKSON'S ROAD TO THE NFL

Copyright © 2017 Bill Lightle

ISBN-13: 978-1979221337
ISBN-10: 1979221332

Published by Bill Lightle
285 Kari Glen Drive
Fayetteville, GA 30215

Contents

*This book is dedicated to these Albany (GA)
High School football coaches in the early 1970s:*

*Ferrell Henry, Phil Spooner, Darrell Willett,
Ronnie Archer, and Willie Magwood.*

FOREWORD

Bobby "Bojack" Jackson's remarkable collegiate career began with a bit of controversy over the second semester senior from Albany, Georgia. The five-foot nine freshman, who might have weighed 170 pounds with rocks in his pockets, was such an outstanding athlete that numerous confrontations between Dan Henning, offensive coordinator, and me occurred frequently prior to the beginning of spring practice at Florida State University in 1974.

Fortunately, he played defense. It took only four or five practice sessions for Bobby to secure a starting position at cornerback – one that he never gave up in four years with the team. He became one of the most outstanding defensive players in the country. As an All-American his senior year, he anchored one of the finest defensive backfields in FSU history. That secondary included Lee Nelson, St. Louis Cardinals; Gary Woolford, New York Giants; Nat Terry, Pittsburgh Steelers; and Joe Camps.

Bobby's late sixth-round selection by the New York Jets in 1978 was not only shocking, but disturbing. His foot-quickness, speed, ball skills, and recovery ability in terms of tackling should have put him into the top three rounds of the draft. Surely his size was the one measurable quality that kept him out of the early rounds. What most failed to realize was the size of his heart. His competitive spirit and work ethic were extraordinary. The New York Jets inherited an eight-year starter at cornerback.

This quiet, unassuming, gifted football player from Albany, Georgia, who started four years at FSU with All-American honors and started eight years in the NFL for the New York

Jets, is the only player I personally know to have accomplished such a thing. Obviously, Bobby's career was remarkable, but his personal character was even more remarkable.

Donald "Deek" Pollard

FSU Defensive Back Coach 1974 & '75

PREFACE

As he waited single file with the other dancers, he listened to the drums as the sun began to rise over the Sioux reservation. Friends and family members had gathered near the dancers, offering prayers intended to give them the strength to complete the grueling, sacred ritual of the Sun Dance.

Bobby Jackson, once one of the great football players for the New York Jets, had come to the endless prairie in the summer of 2010 to challenge himself in a way he had never been challenged before. He had been accepted at the Standing Rock Reservation in South Dakota to participate in the annual Lakota Sun Dance. The dance began with the rising sun.

The dancers awaited the signal to begin , knowing, for those who had the strength and courage to complete the ritual, they would dance four consecutive days, sunup to sundown, without food or water. Four days without food or water. It would be an incredible challenge for any person, even a former NFL standout who, as a player, had always pushed his body and mind for maximum results. On the football field, Bobby had played no other way.

Bobby had sacrificed for years before the Sun Dance in ways that had made him one of the top collegiate and professional football players in the country. Now he had undertaken something much more demanding. Something that would require a level of commitment and sacrifice that he had never given before that summer.

Bobby was once one of the best cornerbacks in the NFL. Through the late 1970s and early 1980s, as he played for the Jets, he had earned a reputation as a ferocious hitter. He played like a warrior and was fearless on the field. More than once he knocked out opposing fullbacks who outweighed him by fifty pounds. He was only five-foot nine and 170 pounds, but those were only numbers. The heart speaks louder than numbers do.

Years after his playing days ended, Bobby confronted something much more dangerous than a charging fullback. He lost the thing that had once made him a premier athlete. He lost self-discipline. His life had spiraled out of control through the use of crack cocaine and experiencing all the dangers of the illegal-drug world.

Part of why he had come to Standing Rock was not only to face the challenge of the Sun Dance, but to seek redemption for past sins. To try to realign his life through native culture.

"Too small to play football in junior high," said the coaches at the school he attended in Albany, Georgia, in the late 1960s. Bobby felt intimidated by what those coaches had said then, but he wouldn't hold that thought long.

When he finally played organized football in high school, he called those junior high coaches, and others who said he was too small to make it big, "dream stealers." By the time he put on a football uniform for the first time as a sophomore at Albany High, he was listening more to himself than to the dream stealers.

After high school he accepted a scholarship to play for Florida State University, started all four years, ended his career with ten interceptions, and was inducted into the FSU Football Hall of Fame in the early 1990s.

In 1978, the Jets drafted him in the sixth round, and he said he was disappointed he didn't go higher, believing the team was hesitant to take him because he was smaller than most professional players. He earned a starting position at cornerback as a rookie in pre-season camp.

Later he became defensive captain, and started for the team from 1978 to 1985. He was selected to the All-Time Jets Team after 21 career interceptions.

His troubles began after his football career ended in 1986 with the Atlanta Falcons. Bobby continued living in New York, where he had married and fathered four children with his wife. Before his marriage in 1983, he had fathered three other children, two out of wedlock. In 2013, he met his child born in 1977 for the first time.

Bobby's personal and family life was strained by his own behavior for several years after football. In the mid-2000s Bobby used crack cocaine and frequently sold the drug to others. He became a drug addict.

Over the years he had affairs with other women while married, and, as the drugs and the philandering created "personal demons" within him, he eventually longed to purge them, he said later. This side of his life few people knew about, especially those back in Albany who had watched him grow up as a respectable boy and a fine young man, and had cheered for him as he played high school football.

By the summer of 2010, when he was accepted as a participant in the Sun Dance, he hoped the ritual would finally help heal him, and help vanquish the demons.

That summer he became the first black man to dance the sacred Lakota Sun Dance at Standing Rock Reservation in South Dakota. Many years before it had been foretold a man with dark skin would one day dance the Sun Dance, the elders at the reservation told him. What was foretold was fulfilled.

Suffering can be the path to spiritual growth, they reminded him. He had prepared himself physically and mentally for the Sun Dance, as much as one can prepare for such an ordeal, and when he left Long Island, New York for the more than thirty-hour drive to the Great Plains, he was ready to dance. He had two incisions, or piercings, of his chest. As part of the ritual, his flesh was cut and blood would flow before the dancing began. Like hitting an NFL fullback head-on out of the backfield, he would have to be willing to accept the pain and sacrifice of the Sun Dance.

The drummers were beating, and the dancers were waiting. As the sun came up over the prairie, the dancing began.

CHAPTER 1

One afternoon some of the boys living in and around the public housing projects in Albany, Georgia, had gathered for their regular football game, usually played in open lots. On this day they found an unlocked gate at Albany High's football stadium. They entered the stadium with both reverence and trepidation. They walked down the concrete steps toward the field.

The boys were silent for a few moments, as if they were in church. Once on the grassy field, they picked sides and played for more than two hours. Sweat and blood sometimes flowed equally. When the game was over that day, most of the talk was about one young, small, but surprisingly tough, player.

They played tackle. They hit hard, but would help one another up after the licks were delivered. These were no games for complainers, those weak of heart. They wore no pads when they played. They were a group of tough kids unafraid to hit or to receive a blow. The game's toughness reflected the neighborhood in which they were coming of age.

They had little money for frills, and sports were more than just games for enjoyment. They were a way to prove yourself to others, a way to make your mark in this world. Some of those boys dreamed of playing college football and even at the professional level. Few would accomplish such goals, but one of the smallest boys there that day did.

During some of those pick-up games of the late 1960s and early '70s, during Bobby Jackson's early teenage years, players sometimes taped coke bottles to their arms to forearm opponents with. Most players wore tennis shoes or rubber cleats, but it was not uncommon to see one or two boys wearing metal cleats. They were not hesitant to purposely step on the feet of their opponents during a play, or when a play ended. There were few rules during these games.

Speed, quickness, and toughness were prized. Bobby had all three. Most of those boys didn't realize it until that day at the stadium.

This particular pick-up game in Albany High's Hugh Mills Stadium, a behemoth of concrete and steel that could seat around eight thousand people, revealed the coming of Bobby Jackson. Football in Albany at that time captivated most young boys, white and black. Bobby was no different.

One of Bobby's friends playing that day was Nathaniel "Big Nate" Henderson, who was about six five and 245 pounds when he graduated from Albany High School in 1974, the same year Bobby did. They were football teammates both at Albany High School and at FSU. The two knew each other in junior high, and became close friends in high school. That day in the stadium during the pick-up game, Bobby was one of the smallest guys on the field, as he usually was.

Some of the guys were two and three years older than Bobby and Nathaniel. Playing against Bobby was Jerry White, who had been a lineman for one of the local high school teams, and was a couple of years older than Bobby.

"He out-weighed Bobby by sixty pounds," Big Nate said.

The play still turns to color in Nathaniel's mind all these years later. Jerry's team had called a running play, with Jerry the lead blocker. Now the play was on. Bobby moved into position to confront both Jerry and the ball carrier. This shouldn't have been good for Bobby because of Jerry's significant size advantage. Bobby seemed over-matched, but not for the first time, or the last.

"Bobby was so much smaller, and he could've been crushed by Jerry," Nathaniel said.

Jerry came bearing down on Bobby and could crush him, setting the runner free. Bobby gave no ground to Jerry and used his excellent balance and surprising strength and determination to fend off the block and tackle the ball carrier. When the play was over, Nathaniel Henderson wasn't the only player at the stadium that day who realized Bobby was going to be special.

*

Bobby's mother, Donna Mae Newsome, was born in 1940 and was only sixteen when she gave birth to him. Donna Mae's family was from Calhoun County, just west of Albany, a rural area known then and still today for farming, forestry, and poverty. Donna Mae's parents, Annie Will and Wilber, had sixteen children, of which fourteen, seven boys and seven girls, lived to adulthood. Two other boys had been born to the couple, but died in infancy.

Their ancestors had been enslaved in the 1800s and picked cotton in Georgia and Alabama. Wilber worked in the pulp wood business in Calhoun County, hauling timber to a sawmill, and was a physically strong, sometimes hot-tempered man, and protective of his children.

Near the family home was a store owned by a white man where black families shopped, and in the back of store the owner sold moonshine and allowed blacks to drink there and play poker. Donna Mae's father once sent one of her sisters to the store to buy a straight razor.

Her sister had a speech impediment, and the owner made fun of her and sent her home without the razor saying, " 'Send me someone who can talk,' " Donna Mae said later.

Wilber Newsome became angry that one of his children had been ridiculed. He went to the store and confronted the owner, and a fistfight ensued.

"Daddy beat the man up pretty bad," Donna Mae said. "My daddy had a temper. He was protective of all of us."

Not long after the fight, Wilber Newsome was given some poison moonshine from the white man's store, drank it, and died.

The incident occurred in 1948, not a time in the South when blacks felt safe reporting to the police a possible crime committed against them by a white person. The family did not contact the police, but were convinced that Wilbur Newsome had been murdered.

"I think he later felt bad for killing daddy," Donna Mae said, "because he used to bring Momma boxes of food from the store after Wilber's death."

At around age fourteen, Donna Mae often played softball with neighborhood friends, and during one game she met Robert Charles Jackson, who lived nearby on Pine Avenue.

Five years older than Donna Mae, after they met Robert told her, " 'Do you know you're one of the prettiest girls I've ever seen?' " Donna Mae said.

He went to Donna Mae's house to ask her mother if he could take her on a date. Her mother at first said no, but then changed her mind when Robert said his mother was Rebecca Jackson, a woman well respected throughout the neighborhood. Robert took Donna Mae to the Ritz Theater downtown and they saw the romantic religious epic *Samson and Delilah*.

The handsome Robert Jackson conducted himself as a "total gentleman and my mother loved him to death," Donna Mae said. "He was my first everything."

Not long after they attended the movie, the couple began living together. They were in love. They sang together each Sunday in the choir at Friendship Baptist Church on Broad Avenue.

In the mid-1950s, Robert Charles Jackson, Sr. received his draft notice from the Army and reported to Fort Jackson in Columbia, South Carolina, for basic training. When Donna Mae, who did not attend high school, was sixteen, Robert returned to Albany on furlough and went to the doctor with Donna Mae and learned that she was pregnant.

He returned to Fort Jackson for a few months, but was given a fifteen-day furlough by the military to be with Donna Mae when she had their baby.

On December 23, 1956, Robert "Bobby" Charles Jackson, Jr. was born at Phoebe Putney Hospital in Albany. Hospital facilities were racially segregated, reflecting the era in which Bobby Jackson was born. Donna Mae turned seventeen on January 13, 1957.

Not long after Bobby was born, the Army stationed Robert Charles Jackson, Sr. in Korea for several months at a time. When Bobby's father was overseas, his mother began frequenting some of the local clubs in Albany, meeting servicemen from the two local military bases. She danced and drank alcohol and had other "new experiences," she said.

Some of the men she met were from the Marine Corps Supply Base. She met Nathaniel Ware from Detroit, who was stationed in Turner Air Force Base in Albany, and became pregnant with his child.

A son, Danny, was born to her and Nathaniel Ware, but that pregnancy and child led to a divorce from Bobby's father in 1959. At one point Robert Jackson, Sr. agreed to remain married to Donna Mae and raise both boys, Bobby and Danny. But Robert's mother, Rebecca Jackson, told her son she would disown him if he did not get a divorce.

"I wish I had gone in another direction" and been true to Bobby's father, Donna Mae said. "Seeing all the pain I put Bobby's father through still hurts even today. I knew we loved each other back then. I know I made some mistakes."

Not long after the divorce, Donna Mae moved to Coca Beach, Florida, with Earl Jerome Greenlee, who had also been stationed at Turner Air Force Base. Greenlee had received a transfer to Cocoa Beach. Donna Mae lived with Greenlee for several years but did not marry him. The couple had two children.

During this period she returned to Albany a few times a year to visit family and spend time with Bobby, who was living with his father and later his grandmother, Rebecca Jackson.

Donna Mae was about eight months pregnant on one of her visits to Albany in 1962. During that visit, national civil rights leader Dr. Martin Luther King, Jr. had come to Albany to help blacks desegregate public facilities. Donna Mae and a friend went to a store to buy a fish sandwich. On the way there, she realized Dr. King was in the same neighborhood speaking through a bullhorn telling blacks about upcoming efforts in the local civil rights movement known as the Albany Movement.

The police arrived with a paddy wagon and begin to arrest some of the marchers who were following Dr. King. One officer used his club to strike Donna Mae in the face.

"All I wanted was a fish sandwich," she said. She was not jailed, as were many blacks that protested the racist policies of the city and the South during this period.

In September 1962, *U. S. News & World Report* published a story on the ongoing racial unrest in Albany. At that time, whites outnumbered blacks about thirty-six thousand to twenty thousand, the story reported. Whites controlled the local industries, while two large federal payrolls, Turner Air Force Base and the Marine Corps Supply Center, were feeding the local economy. The federal government was also being petitioned by those in the Albany Movement to end racial segregation in public facilities.

Lawsuits had been filed requesting the government to desegregate bus lines and train depots, libraries, parks, playgrounds, swimming pools, theaters, the municipal auditorium, recreation centers for teenagers, toilet facilities, and schools. The story went on to report:

> Before the Negro campaign began last year, Albany was considered a rather moderate Southern city. There had been a

minimum of racial trouble. A Negro once held the elective office of coroner. There had been little activity by the Ku Klux Klan or White Citizens Council – even during the recent racial disturbances. The climate of race relations began to heat up early in 1961, when Negroes stepped up their demands for desegregation.

Violence against blacks in Albany during this period included law officers attacking pregnant women. Mrs. Slater King was visiting a prisoner in the Camilla jail, about twenty miles south of Albany, when a deputy sheriff attacked her. Pregnant at the time, but as a result of the attack, she lost her baby. Mrs. King's brother-in-law was Albany attorney C. B. King, who provided legal representation for those arrested during the Albany Movement.

King himself was once beaten with a cane while seeing clients in Albany at the Dougherty County Jail. Later, Sheriff Cull Campbell said, "Yeah, I knocked the hell out of that son-of-a-bitch, and I'd do it again. I wanted to let him know . . . I'm a white man and he's a damn nigger."

During this same violent and troubled period, *Newsweek* magazine reporters interviewed Albany Police Chief Laurie Pritchett. "There are three things I like to do," Pritchett said. "Drink buttermilk, put niggers in jail, and kick reporters' asses."

*

While visiting Bobby in Albany, Donna Mae noticed that when he played football in the streets or in neighborhood yards, Bobby ran faster than other boys. A lot faster. She noticed something else. Bobby was not the rowdy type or the "rough gangster type. He was more like his daddy, a lady's man," she said. "He had a nice smile and easy manner. Kind of shy at times."

Other boys, she realized back then, were even jealous because he was more handsome than most, and the girls were attracted to him.

Usually Donna Mae came four or five times a year and stayed several days, visiting her family and son in Albany. During one such visit, when Bobby was around six years old, his parents were together and, although his father had remarried, the couple was holding hands.

Bobby became hopeful that they might get back together, that he would get to live with both his father and mother, Donna Mae said. But it did not happen.

"I remember seeing them walking together and holding hands," Bobby said. "I was thinking we'd all be together again. I was just a little boy."

After his parents divorced, Bobby's father married Laverne Moore, who had been a contemporary of Donna Mae's. "They knew each other growing up," Bobby said. "There was competition between them over my dad."

During one of Donna Mae's visits to see Bobby, an argument between Donna Mae and Laverne erupted because Laverne refused to let Donna Mae see her son. Bobby's father got between the two women to prevent a physical fight, Donna Mae said.

"I was coming after her," Donna Mae said. "No one was going to keep me away from my own son. I got a temper and Bobby gets his from me." She eventually visited Bobby.

By the mid-1960s, Donna Mae's relationship with Earl Jerome Greenlee had ended, and she met and later married James Meeks . Meeks worked as a chef in Coca Beach, Florida, but he and Bobby's mother moved to the Los Angeles area, where he found a job in the same line of work. Donna Mae became pregnant and returned to Albany in 1967 to have the child, because the hospital costs for childbirth were less expensive in Albany than in California, she said.

She had a son, James Meeks Jr., but the boy would never know his father. A few weeks after James' birth, his father was shot dead by a white woman in California who he had been having an affair with, Donna Mae said. Later, Donna Mae returned to California, and it would be years before she saw her first son, Bobby Jackson, again.

She made no effort to reach out to Bobby. No telephone calls, no letters. He did not know where she was, or who she was with, for years. She did not attend any of his high school or college football games. She knew about his successes on the football field from speaking with her family members in Albany.

She said she did not worry about him during this period because she knew he received good care from his father and other family members.

"I thought about him a lot," she said. "But I was trying to find a life for me and my other children."

Bobby longed to see his mother and remained hurt by her absence. He later accepted her apology for the almost twelve years of neglect. Her next contact with Bobby came by happenstance in Long Island, New York, in the late 1970s. She was unaware her son played for the New York Jets.

*

Bobby had a troubled relationship with his stepmother, Laverne Moore. Bobby's father and his stepmother had one child together, David. Bobby's struggles began then. His stepmother overtly favored David over Bobby, causing Bobby both anguish and insecurity, he said. He did not feel loved by her. Just the opposite of what he felt when he visited his paternal grandmother.

Bobby found the love, discipline, and kindness every boy needs from Rebecca Jackson, who lived on Pine Avenue in Albany. Next door to his grandmother lived Rozelle Jackson, his great-grandmother and matriarch of the family. Both were women of strength and deep faith in God, Bobby said.

Bobby liked being around both women, and he felt safe and loved in their presence. When he visited their neighborhood, Bobby played with the boys living there, especially his cousin, Charlie Johnson, who later became one of Bobby's football teammates at Albany High.

He longed to live with his grandmother and wanted out of the home with his father, stepmother, and brother, David. At the end of his second grade year at Lincoln Heights Elementary, where he became an honor roll student, Bobby did something that eventually led him to his grandmother's house.

Bobby had "fallen in love," he said, with his second-grade teacher, Ms. Hudson. He planned to do something special for her at the end of the school year to show her how much he cared about her. Some boys and girls give their favorite teachers fruit, cakes, and maybe a pretty handkerchief. But little Bobby had bigger plans than a handkerchief. His love was big.

"I took my stepmother's wedding ring and wrapped it up and gave it to Ms. Hudson," Bobby said. "This was during the last week of school. I was in love with her."

Ms. Hudson contacted Bobby's stepmother and returned the ring. His stepmother was furious.

"She beat the crap out of me," Bobby said. "I don't remember if she used a belt or just her hand or something else. I just remember her beating me. At that point I didn't want any part of her."

What should've been viewed as an act of innocent boyhood infatuation had been met with outrage, instead.

Still, Bobby sought to leave his father's house. After the whipping, he talked with his father, who was empathetic to his son's predicament. Unable to change his wife's behavior toward Bobby, the elder Jackson arranged for him to live with his grandmother, Rebecca Jackson. Bobby lived with her until he graduated from high school in 1974 and left Albany to attend FSU.

Rebecca provided the proper balance of love, kindness, and discipline that shaped Bobby's formative years. She acted as mother, father, and grandmother all in one, and made sure

Bobby went to school each day and to church every Sunday, he said. They attended Friendship Baptist and, later, First Bethesda. She was a disciplinarian and expected her grandson to behave, respect others, and do his best in whatever he decided to do with his life.

His grandmother lived in a fragile wooden house with a tin roof that leaked during a hard rain. She paid seven dollars a week rent for the home at 725 Pine Avenue, a few blocks from downtown Albany. In the two houses next to Rebecca's lived Bobby's great-grandmother Rozelle Jackson, and his cousin Charlie Johnson.

In Bobby's new home, the living room also served as his bedroom. There was no central heat or air conditioning, but they had electricity. During cold nights, Bobby loaded the wood stove with split pieces of oak, providing heat for him and his grandmother. They had a toilet and running water inside the house, but no bathtub or shower. When Bobby bathed, his grandmother heated water on the stove and poured it into a large, round metal tub, and Bobby got in the tub with soap and washcloth.

"If I wasn't real dirty, sometimes I'd just stand over the sink and use a wash cloth to bathe," Bobby said.

Rebecca used a washing machine with hand-operated rollers to wash clothes, and a clothesline in their backyard to dry them. As Bobby became older, his grandmother took their clothes to a nearby laundromat to wash and dry them with modern appliances.

"I never lacked for love or food," Bobby said. "But when I went to other people's houses I said, 'Hey, they make houses out of bricks, too?'"

Bobby and his cousin Charlie Johnson, just a little older than Bobby, spent a lot of time together in the neighborhood. "We were poor and didn't know we were poor," Charlie said.

They played pick-up tackle football games with other boys. No uniforms or padding were worn during these games. The boys hit each other hard. When they were about ten years old, the two had separate teams, each composed of about five or six regular players. Bobby became captain of his team, the Oakland Raiders, and Charlie captain of the Kansas City Chiefs. The two teams played in nearby vacant lots.

Bobby played quarterback and often became upset if one of his teammates missed a pass from him. It bothered him a great deal when he lost, Charlie said, unlike most of the other boys.

"He had a winning mentality and a fiery temper," Charlie said. "He'd bring out the best in you if you were on his team, and he was always the fastest kid out there."

On Sundays after the cousins attended Friendship Baptist Church, they played on a field off Highland Avenue, a few blocks from their homes. Other groups of black boys from east Albany came to play as well. Blacks during that period, following the segregated traditions of the city, lived in the east and southern parts of the city. Whites in the north and west. Bobby and Charlie played with the CME Hellcats.

CME referred to a housing project, and the letters indicated the Christian Methodist Episcopal Church. Bobby and other boys called it Crime, Murder, and Execution.

Other teams included the Highland Bears and the River Rats, a team from east of the Flint River. Bobby lived on the west side of the Flint.

"Those were tough games where the kids would try to knock your head off," Charlie said. "Bobby looked like the pretty boy who would get the girl, but on the field he played like a man."

The Pine Avenue neighborhood where Bobby grew up included many close families that "looked out for one another," Charlie said.

"Some people drank a lot on the weekends," Charlie said. "I even remember some moonshine. But it was a pretty safe place back then. People watched out for each other. There was a lot of love in that neighborhood."

Charlie and Bobby slept outside on cool summer evenings, looked up at the stars and talked about girls, football, and the latest music. They dreamed of being professional football players, being famous and making lots of money. Sometimes they dreamed about pretty girls. They had the same dreams a lot of boys did in their neighborhood.

Bobby and Charlie both said they were more like brothers than cousins. Not the kind of brothers that fought and didn't like one another. Just the opposite. They were always together playing in their neighborhood because they liked one another, had similar interests, and felt secure with each other. Charlie called Bobby, "Doo Da Bug," and Bobby's nickname for Charlie was "Plute."

Bobby got his nickname from his grandmother, who called him Doo Da Bug because he was constantly moving, whether inside the house or outside. He had enough childhood energy for three boys instead of one, family members said.

"My grandmother was always getting on to me about not getting into things when I was inside," he said. "I guess it was hard for me to stay still back then."

Charlie spent a lot of time at Bobby's house, where Rebecca Jackson often baked delicious pound cakes and played albums by soul singer Aretha Franklin.

"Bobby's grandmother was a sweet lady," Charlie said. "We used to say she was kind of mean," but she was providing discipline for Bobby.

Once, when Bobby was about nine, a hard rain came and Rebecca told her grandson to stay inside until the rain ended, then he could play outside. Bobby did not do what he was told to do. He left the house, crossed Pine Avenue, got soaked, and returned home. When Rebecca saw him, she became furious and told Bobby he was going to get a whipping because he had disobeyed her.

Bobby had gotten whippings from her before, usually with a bundle of switches from a bush or tree that she would make him collect and bring to her. Bobby ran out of the house when he heard about the whipping. But his older cousin by several years, Bill Jackson, knew what was happening and caught Bobby as he was trying to run away.

"I didn't get far," Bobby said. "I tried to fake him out, but he caught me between our houses."

Bill took Bobby back to his grandmother, and Bobby got a hard spanking from her. Bobby respected Bill, who spent time encouraging Bobby to do the right thing and be respectful to others, especially his grandmother.

"Bill was always looking after me," Bobby said. "He had a big influence on me when I lived on Pine Avenue. I looked up to him."

Usually when Rebecca whipped Bobby it was with switches, and occasionally a belt, while he kept his pants on. One time, she made Bobby take off all of his clothes before she administered the punishment.

"I don't remember what I did that time," Bobby said. "I'm sure I deserved it. She expected me to do what she told me to do. She was trying to give me discipline. She loved me."

*

Both Bobby and Charlie attended Carver Junior High School, located at West Mercer Avenue and South Monroe Street, a few blocks from their homes. Carver was an all-black school, seventh through ninth grades. "Bobby was smaller than most boys his age, but also better looking," Charlie said.

"He got a lot of attention from the girls," Charlie said, "It made a lot of other boys jealous." Bobby also got the attention of some of the school bullies, who took cookies, milk, and even lunch money from other students.

They picked on Bobby because of his height and called him "pretty boy," Charlie said. On some days the bullies threatened to beat Bobby up at the end of the school day. Bobby always had a plan. When the final bell rang, he would run out the school door and all the way home to his grandmother.

"Bobby was not a fighter," Charlie said. "He didn't have to be because the bullies could never catch him."

CHAPTER 2

Rebecca Jackson came into the world in 1915 as part of a sharecropping family in Baker County, Georgia. Like most poor black families in Baker, her family farmed land owned by whites. They worked hard for little money and under terrible conditions, as did most blacks in the South during the first half of the twentieth century.

As a child she picked cotton by hand, but attended a few years of formal schooling, family members said. By the mid-1930s, she had given birth to three children, fathered by three different men. She never married. Bobby's father was her oldest child, born in 1935.

Sparsely populated Baker County, created in 1825, is about twenty miles south of Albany. Like much of the land throughout southwest Georgia during that period and leading up to the outbreak of the Civil War in 1861, Baker County had large cotton plantations that used black slaves to do the work.

After slavery ended in 1865 and through the next hundred years, sharecropping replaced slavery, as blacks suffered violence at the hands of white supremacists in Baker County. By the time of the national Civil Rights Movement in the 1950s and 1960s, blacks seeking justice and equality in the county often referred to it as "Bad Baker" because of the violence they had endured.

Many poor blacks and poor whites, during the first part of the twentieth century in the South, sought to escape the hardscrabble life of sharecropping. Some went to Northern cities and found jobs in factories, and others went to the closest Southern cities looking for better opportunities. Not long after all three of her children were born, Rebecca Jackson moved from rural Baker County to Albany.

In Albany she worked as a domestic in the homes of white families. She cleaned, cooked, and took care of children. The money wasn't much, but better than she earned for the life-crushing work of picking cotton ten hours a day or longer.

Bobby's father completed a few years of schooling, but did not graduate from high school. As a young man in Albany he delivered the statewide newspaper, the *Atlanta Constitution.* After being drafted by the Army in the mid-1950s, his father spent about ten years in the military and was honorably discharged as part of the U.S. Army Corps of Engineers.

Throughout his life, Bobby maintained a good relationship with his father, who nicknamed him "Snoop" when he was a young boy. Bobby doesn't remember how the name came about, but most likely because he was always moving and getting into things.

Bobby does remember learning from his father the importance of a solid work ethic. As a junior high student, his dad took him and his stepbrother David with him on weekends when he made extra money cleaning business offices in town.

Those weekends with his father established a pattern of hard work that later transferred to the football field and in the weight room, Bobby said.

"I idolized my dad," Bobby said. "I wanted to be just like him."

While living with his grandmother, Bobby spent the weekends at his father's house where he could bathe in his dad's bathtub instead of the metal tub at his grandmother's house.

"That was a big deal to me," Bobby said. "I would stay in the tub as long as I wanted."

Around the mid-1960s after leaving the Army, Bobby's dad began working for Southern Bell Company, where he spent several years as a lineman and in other capacities. Unlike Bobby, his father had not been an athlete growing up. No one in the family remembers any evidence of the elder Jackson showing outstanding foot-speed as his son did early on.

Family members recalled Bobby's father, who died in 2004, as a "soft-spoken" man, but when he spoke people listened to him.

Robert Charles Jackson, Sr. had a fine singing voice and helped form a gospel group called Southern Quintet. The group sang at churches in and around Albany. People considered him handsome, he dressed well, and he easily made friends, family members said. Bobby wanted to be like him in those ways, he said.

The marriage between Bobby's father and stepmother, La-verne Moore, soon turned argumentative and ended in divorce by the mid-1960s. Bobby's father would not re-marry after his second divorce.

*

On one of Donna Mae's trips to Albany after she had left Bobby and moved to Florida, she brought two of her other children with her. Bobby, nine or ten and playing at a neigh-borhood park, saw a boy and a girl who looked familiar. They looked like Bobby from a distance. He approached the pair for a better look. As he got closer, both of them indeed looked like Bobby, with the same eyes and facial features.

"I went up to them and said, 'Who's your mother?' They said, 'Donna Mae.' And then I said, 'She's mine too.' "

*

Instead of sports at Carver Junior High, Bobby played the drums in the band. Outside of school he also played drums in a band called Soul Dells. Ernest Worthy, one of Bobby's class-mates and friends, formed the band. Ernest played guitar and they played songs by James Brown, known as the Godfather of Soul, and other groups like the Temptations. They played for anybody who would listen, especially girls. Bobby became a good drummer, and the music became a stepping-stone to meet girls. Ernest and Bobby also played sandlot football together and became teammates at Albany High in the early 1970s.

At Carver Junior High, Bobby focused on the band and his schoolwork, and earned praise from some of his teachers, including Mrs. Ruby Hampton, who taught English.

"My grandmother made sure I went to school well-dressed," Bobby said. "And that I did my homework and respected my teachers."

Mrs. Hampton taught for thirty-four years in the Albany/Dougherty County public schools. Born in 1931, she earned degrees from Bennett College in Greensboro, North Carolina, and from Albany State College.

"Bobby was a good student," Mrs. Hampton said. "He was shy, mild-mannered, and conscientious. He always wanted to please. I taught his daddy. He was just like his daddy."

At Carver, Bobby developed close relationships with a group of students that included Brian Hampton, Mrs. Hampton's son; Melvin Rambeau; Eugene Richardson; and Marcus Hines, Mrs. Hampton said. She said they were a good group of boys, who had fun, were respectful, and "never got into serious trouble and were enjoyable to be around."

Mrs. Hampton said she challenged her students by having them write poetry and essays about their own personal interests. She said she wanted them to understand the importance of writing clearly and in complete sentences. Bobby became one of her top students and earned a B plus in her class.

She described him as small, and he didn't carry a lot of weight. She never noticed Bobby expressing any interest in athletics. If she had seen Bobby before the school day began, she would have seen a different side of him.

Before classes began at Carver, Bobby gathered in the schoolyard with a group of boys, most of whom played on the school's football team, and played touch football. They used an empty milk carton full of rocks as a football. Among those he played with were Marvin Trice and Richard Baker, two of the many fine athletes who came out of Carver and became top basketball and football players at the local high schools.

"Most of those guys were just a lot bigger than me," he said.

During his ninth-grade year and through these before-school football games, he developed confidence about his own ability to compete. "At that point I knew I was a good athlete," even though he was smaller than most of the boys he played with, Bobby said.

Bobby grew fond of Mrs. Hampton and has remained that way over the years, forever thankful for her guidance and teaching.

"She was special to me and a lot of kids back then," Bobby said. "She made us work hard in class and behave. She was always supportive."

In 2013, when his number 45 became the first to be retired from Albany High, Bobby asked Mrs. Hampton to attend the ceremony at the stadium. She sat there that night with Bobby's close friends and family members, supporting him during the ceremony at Hugh Mills Stadium. The stadium is a place where many times in the early 1970s he thrilled crowds with his brilliant speed, tenacious hitting, and supreme desire to excel.

She said she had been proud of him and his success, but his accomplishments were not unpredictable.

"I went to a few of his games at Albany High," she said. "I was surprised he was participating in football. Not surprised he was good. He just didn't look like a football player in junior high, but I knew whatever he was going to do, he was going to be good at it."

*

Bobby became good at one thing in particular – running. He proved this not only on the sandlot football field countless times, but also by racing the city garbage trucks as they came through his neighborhood on summer mornings. Usually there were a handful of other boys hiding with him in an alley near his home on Pine Avenue. Some were fast, but none of them as fast as Bobby.

They knew when and where the trucks were coming. They waited and plotted and hid behind shrubs and trees along the dirt alley. Intense competition can take many forms. Once a garbage truck passed them, they ran hard, but only one would catch it.

"They all tried to catch it," Bobby said. "I was usually the only one that could." Occasionally Charlie Johnson, Bobby's cousin, caught the garbage truck, but he fell off hard onto the ground, unable to keep his grip long.

"I couldn't do it the way Bobby did," Charlie said. "No one could. But I did catch it a couple of times."

Bobby developed the superb timing he used on a football field by running after and jumping to grab an iron rail on a garbage truck. He'd ride for about a hundred yards and when the truck turned, jump off, able to keep his balance and keep running. No other boy could do it the way he did.

Speed, jumping ability, balance, and great determination, all symbolized his football career. And all crowned him king of the garbage trucks.

Growing up, Bobby met Johnny "Mule" Coleman, who was a year older and had earned his nickname from the animal-like manner in which he hit opposing football players. Before Bobby began playing organized football, he used to ask Johnny, "Why do you hit people so hard?" And Johnny would say to Bobby, "That's the only way I know how to play. That's how you earn respect. Make the other team fear you."

Johnny grew up with older brothers who could be tough on him, and he had to be tough back, if he was to survive. For the three years I played football at Albany High, Johnny and

Bobby were two of the hardest hitters there among other tough ball players. When they made solid licks, sometimes head-to-head as was within the rules then, it sounded like a high-speed car crash. The sound of it scared me. The way Mule hit on the football field intimidated players if their hearts were weak. He'd frighten his own teammates. Bobby eventually hit the same way.

Bobby and Johnny shared another quality. They had an easy demeanor off the field. They were not arrogant or boastful. They played sandlot together, and Johnny, along with Charlie Johnson, finally convinced Bobby to join the Albany High School football team in 1971. Johnny remembered Bobby this way during some of those early sandlot games, before Bobby played organized football for the first time at Albany High.

"He was just a little scrawny athlete," Johnny said. "We ran everywhere together in the neighborhood. He was shy at times and doubted he could play."

His confidence grew the more he played neighborhood football. During the summer of 1971, as the two boys hung out together, Johnny began to talk to him at length about playing football at Albany High. Bobby began to listen and consider going out for the team.

Bobby became aware of Albany High's notorious two-week pre-season August camp, conducted in the woods a few miles outside of Albany along the Muckalee Creek. Graves Springs Football Camp was located off Graves Springs Road in nearby Lee County. It had been the site of Albany High's pre-season camp since the 1930s.

During that decade four Albany businessmen, H. E. "Yank" Davis, F. B. "Wig" Wiggins, Maurice Tift, and E. H. Kalmon, financially helped the high school acquire about fifty acres of property along the Muckalee Creek, isolated in the woods, then and now, just off Graves Springs Road, a few miles from Albany High School.

The *Albany Herald* published stories referring to these men, who were passionate about football, as the "Four Horsemen," a moniker of biblical origins that had gained national attention when associated with the runaway gallop of the Notre Dame backfield. Albany's own Horsemen not only secured a new training camp for the high school team, but also financed banquets at the downtown Gordon Hotel to honor the school's teams.

At the 1937 banquet given by the Horsemen, the principal speaker was Russell Lake, athletic director and head football coach at Mercer University in Macon, Georgia. The *Herald's* headline in connection with the story was a quote attributed to Lake concerning Albany High's head coach Harold McNabb: "McNabb Greatest High School Coach in State." Lake went on to say this about football: "I do believe that boys who play football never become a social problem to the community. They learn the creed of sportsmanship on the field and carry it with them throughout the rest of their lives."

By the 1970s, there were three buildings on the Graves Springs training site and three daily practices, usually with no water breaks, even when the temperature reached close to a hundred degrees. Bobby was hesitant to commit to high school football and the tortuous Graves Springs Camp.

The camp began in mid-August, a couple of weeks before school started. Bobby didn't make the decision to go out for the team until camp had ended and school had begun. Still, there was trepidation. He continued to talk with Johnny Coleman and Charlie Johnson, needing their constant encouragement.

Johnny helped Bobby work on his defensive technique in terms of footwork, taking a proper angle to make a tackle, and other insights he had learned on the field. Bobby was eager to learn. At the first few practices, Bobby was still hesitant, but began to relax more after Johnny told him to pretend practice was like playing pick-up games in the housing project, but with a helmet and pads. This encouragement helped Bobby adjust.

His confidence grew during the early practices once school began, and he came to enjoy his B-team year playing cornerback under Coach Willie Magwood. By the end of the year he had earned a reputation as a hard-hitting player with exceptional speed and grit. Bobby quickly came to respect and appreciate Coach Magwood, one of a handful of coaches at Albany High who helped Bobby mature, and molded him for things to come.

In 1970 Willie Magwood became the first black coached hired by Albany High, a school that had an all-white student body until federal court-ordered desegregation allowed a handful of blacks to attend for the first time in 1964. Magwood, Bobby's first coach, instilled in him a sense of the values of fairness, hard work, and respect for the game. He reiterated the values Bobby had been taught at home by his grandmother.

Magwood ensured Bobby and others under him understood no one player is more important than the team as a whole. When you sacrifice, you sacrifice for the team. Magwood was a soft-spoken coach, and he rarely got loud. He kept a close-trimmed Afro and wore green or orange, the team's colors, coaching shirt, shorts, and white athletic socks.

Players and students respected him, and most enjoyed his company. He carried himself in an easy manner, endearing himself to others.

Born in 1943 in Colquitt County, Georgia, about forty miles southeast of Albany, Magwood picked cotton as a boy, up to ten hours a day. He earned two-and-half dollars a day if he picked a hundred pounds. He was one of nine children, but his father died when he was eight, and like his siblings, Willie had to work to help the family financially.

"I got a lot of whippins' from my mother 'cause I didn't pick a hundred pounds," Magwood said.

To escape the punishing work in the fields, Magwood attended Albany State College on an athletic scholarship and played both basketball and football.

In the late 1950s, at around fifteen, Magwood and a group of friends were playing basketball on an outside court. A white woman in a convertible drove by during the game and caught the attention of one of the players, who whistled at her. A seemingly harmless gestured by today's standards could get a black boy killed then by a white mob.

In 1955, a fourteen-year-old black boy from Chicago, Emmitt Till, was murdered by white men while visiting relatives in Mississippi. Till had either whistled or said "hi baby," or possibly both, to a white woman who worked in a store. The woman's husband and half-brother became so enraged that they kidnapped Till, beat him, and then shot him before tossing his body into a river.

Fortunately, this did not happen to Magwood's teammate. Not long after the white woman drove by, police officers surrounded the basketball court. The boy who whistled at her was arrested and forced to pay a fine before being released by the police.

Magwood's mother had always taught him to respect all people, white and black, but many times back then it could be difficult, he said.

After graduating from college, Magwood worked briefly for two different high schools before head Coach Ferrell Henry hired him at Albany High, where he eventually coached and taught physical education for thirty years. He never moved to Albany, but made the drive daily from Moultrie, the county seat of Colquitt. He is fondly remembered by Bobby, myself, and many others who played for him on the B-team football and basketball teams.

He soon became a favorite among the entire student body. In 1974, Magwood was one of about ten black teachers at Albany High and became the first black to receive the dedication from the *Thronteeska*, the school's yearbook.

"I was very proud and surprised," Magwood said, "because it was an all-white staff" on the yearbook that made the decision. The dedication page read: "To one who has given time, thought, and effort to Albany High without counting cost . . . Whose smile has often brightened the day for all of us."

*

Willie Magwood did for the Albany High coaching staff what Grady Caldwell had done for the team in 1965 when he became its first black player. Race, how blacks and whites could be teammates and get along with one another, was in Bobby's thoughts in the summer of 1971 as he approached high school. Up to that point he had attended all-black schools.

Race remained in the minds of those who lived in Albany, both black and white. The city was created in the mid-1830s along the Flint River by whites taking large swaths of rich, fertile land – once inhabited by the Creek Indians – planting cotton, and bringing in slaves to do the work. A few whites profited handsomely from the cruel and barbaric nature of chattel slavery. Many more whites, during and after slavery, lived impoverished lives. Here, with the high concentration of African slaves, the Cotton Kingdom took shape. The pillars of the kingdom rested on human bondage.

When the Civil War ended slavery in 1865, Albany's white political leadership eventually created, as did other southern cities, a highly segregated culture. Bobby was born into this culture, but by the time he was headed for Albany High the walls of racial division had begun to crumble.

As a little boy, if Bobby had gone to the public pool at Tift Park, named after the city's founder, Nelson Tift, he would've been denied admission. Had he gone to the public library to check out a book, he would not have been allowed inside. White and colored public facilities characterized the city, as they did across the Deep South.

Racial segregation encompassed the city. But the Civil Rights Movement of the 1960s, and federal legislation faithfully enforced, were breaking racial barriers in Albany and throughout the South.

Before Bobby entered Albany High as a sophomore, an event occurred at the school's football stadium indicating strong white resistance in Albany and throughout the South to the impending racial changes. In September 1968, three years before Bobby played in Hugh Mills Stadium and dazzled spectators, thousands went there to hear a political speech by former Alabama governor, George Wallace, who was running for president.

Wallace's American Independent Party vilified blacks while he urged the nation to uphold the South's history of racial segregation. The crowd included local and state political leaders and a sea of white faces. Lester Maddox, governor of Georgia, attended the rally. A few years before the event in Albany, while Wallace was governor of Alabama, he stood in a doorway at the University of Alabama to deny entrance to black students. President John F. Kennedy's administration ended the standoff by mobilizing troops from the Alabama National Guard to assist federal officials. Wallace eventually stepped away from the door, and the university became desegregated.

Maddox introduced Wallace to the crowd at Hugh Mills Stadium that day, calling the federal government a "gestapo," in reference to Nazi Germany of the 1930s, for passing laws aimed to provide equal opportunities for blacks in the South and throughout the nation.

"Only George Wallace had the courage to identify himself with the rights of the common people," Maddox said, igniting a great cheer throughout the stadium. He meant the common white man, of course. Republican Richard Nixon won the

1968 presidential election, but Wallace won the electoral vote in a handful of southern states, including Georgia.

The Albany High that Bobby attended had been built in the 1950s along Residence Avenue, stretching a full block. Built of red brick, the school had a fine auditorium, gym, tennis courts, and a football practice field next to the imposing Hugh Mills Stadium, named after an earlier coach. And the school could accommodate around eighteen hundred white students.

There had been some racial fights and ugly harassment of black students by whites during the desegregation period of the mid-1960s. But by the time Bobby arrived, the student body was about a thousand, with about seventy-five percent white and the remainder black. During the early 1970s, a calmness and acceptance between the races at school had replaced the tension and overt acts of racism by whites that once existed.

Bobby turned again to his friend Johnny "Mule" Coleman, already a student there, for advice.

"The first time he came out for the team he asked me about blacks and whites getting along on the field and off," Johnny said.

Johnny told him both on and off the field blacks and whites were not only getting along at school, but rejecting the racial history that once defined the city. A new day had begun, despite what George Wallace and Lester Maddox had said in Albany High's football stadium three years earlier.

Johnny was selected the Most Valuable Player for the 1972 Albany High School team. He graduated the following year, joined the Marines, and served three years. Then he became part of the civilian work force at the Marine Base in Albany before retiring after thirty years. He lives in Albany today, and when Bobby returns, which is often, he makes a point to see the friend of his youth, the one who helped him grow in confidence on the football field.

On one visit years ago, Bobby gave Johnny a football he had intercepted from Miami Dolphin quarterback Dan Marino.

"It was a way of saying thanks to Johnny for all the help he had given me," Bobby said. "He helped me a lot back then when I first started playing football at Albany High."

Johnny told Bobby that coaches at Albany High ensured blacks and whites who came out for the team not only got along but "become like a family." The teams of the early 1970s were composed of about thirty white players and roughly twenty blacks. Bobby learned that what Johnny had told him about the races playing together as a team and getting along was true. While blacks and whites didn't regularly socialize after school, a sense of school pride in the hallways and on the athletic fields became a shared value for both races.

"I was just going to a school for the first time that was integrated," Bobby said. "Looking back, I can't remember any problems at school because of race."

Before he entered high school, Bobby had had little contact with whites, and carried within him no prejudicial views toward them, he said. While growing up he did befriend one young white boy whose father owned a gas station not far from Bobby's house. The station sold go-carts, and the boy's father allowed Bobby to ride them with his son.

"We got along together and had fun," Bobby said.

At around the same period, his grandmother, Rebecca Jackson, worked as a domestic for a white family that often gave toys to her that she in turn gave to Bobby. The family had treated her fairly, Bobby said. And his grandmother taught him to be fair and respectful to all people regardless of race.

Bobby carried this lesson with him to Albany High in the fall of 1971. There he would grow as a leader and an athlete, and he played under coaches who instilled in him a desire to improve and to sacrifice for the team.

CHAPTER 3

Around the time Bobby had decided to play football at Albany High, boys in his neighborhood were organizing a race to determine who was the fastest. His reputation as a sprinter had grown, and now the boys who knew him wanted to test him.

They pitted Bobby against James Jones, a year or two older than Bobby. Many considered Jones one of the fastest athletes in the city, and he drew admiration from the boys coming of age in and around the public housing projects. Bobby knew about Jones and looked up to him as well.

Another speedster who Bobby admired when he was growing up was Lester Sherman, a running back at Monroe High who went on to play at Albany State College. Lester Sherman and James Jones were two of the top runners in the city in the 1960s.

"I watched both those guys growing up," Bobby said, "I wanted to be like them. They both had great speed."

Bets were taken on the race between Bobby and James Jones. A crowd of about twenty-five had gathered the day of the race along a vacant lot on the corner of Flint Avenue and Davis Street. That lot was routinely used by Bobby and other boys to play tackle football. It was not uncommon to see two games occurring at the same time on that corner. One game would include young boys, those around ten and eleven years old. The other game was for boys a few years older. They were tough boys who hit hard and didn't complain when they received the same.

"Some of the young kids wanted to graduate to the other side," Charlie Johnson said. "But it was tough over there. You had to be ready to get knocked around a lot."

Charlie remembered the day of the big race.

Across the street from the field was a cinderblock store that sold groceries to black families. Some folks would later refer to it as the Corner Club, a place to buy and drink beer and play cards. Bobby was nervous leading up to the race, but the feeling passed when the race began.

About a hundred yards were marked off, and the two lined up. The signal to start was given and they took off. They were even for the first several yards, then Bobby began to pull away from Jones, beating him by a couple of steps.

"There were some boys surprised Bobby won," Charlie said. "I wasn't. I knew how fast he had gotten."

Jones wanted a rematch and Bobby gave him one. Bobby won again. Jones asked for a third race and got one. Bobby won that one, too.

"I beat him each time," Bobby said. "And now here I am the fastest man in CME. That was a pretty big deal back then. There were a lot of fast guys in that neighborhood."

Around the time Bobby beat James Jones, he and his grandmother moved from their home on Pine Avenue to 671 Society Avenue, part of CME, the public housing neighborhoods near Albany High. From Bobby's new home, he could see the school's imposing football stadium.

Boys from rival public housing projects often settled their disputes with their fists. Not generally guns or knives. Bobby usually didn't get into any fights growing up, and the few he became involved in were usually over girls.

"I knew guys from other housing projects, and it could be very territorial when it came to girls," Bobby said. "We didn't want boys from other areas messing with girls from CME. That's just the way it was."

At his new home, unlike the one he left on Pine Avenue, Bobby had his own bedroom, central air and heat, and a built-in bathtub and shower. The first thing Bobby did when he walked into his new home was to lie down in the bathtub with his clothes on.

"It was like heaven to me," he said.

What the boys in CME knew about Bobby's brilliant speed, head varsity football coach Ferrell Henry at Albany High would soon realize. In the spring of 1972, Bobby's sophomore year, he was part of the school's track team coached by Phil Spooner. Henry, a linebacker, and Spooner, a running back, had played together at FSU in the early 1960s.

In 1972, Spooner told Henry about a B-team football player showing tremendous speed on the track team. Spooner, always looking for new football talent, urged Henry to come watch Bobby run. To come see for himself.

"I began to watch Bobby at track meets," Henry said. "He was so dang little. Maybe 145 pounds, five-eight or five-nine, but you could tell he had potential and courage when he ran. There was something different about him and it just wasn't his speed."

That spring Henry, who had been a high school coach since the mid-1960s, saw something at a track meet that, up to that point, he rated as the greatest high school sporting event he had ever seen. In telling the story in 2014 at his home in Cordele, Georgia, he couldn't recall exactly where Bobby had competed that day.

Bobby, positioned last as part of the four-man mile relay team, got the baton about thirty-five yards behind the leader. Watching Bobby take the baton, Henry realized immediately that he possessed something special. After several yards Bobby had cut into the lead, but Henry said he didn't think he could win the race because of how much he was behind when he started.

Bobby kept pushing, kept making up ground. The crowd sensed something special. The cheers for Bobby grew. Then louder still.

"As he got closer to the finish line," Henry said, "he found another gear and won the race. I had never seen anything like it before or since."

Throughout high school, coaches consistently clocked Bobby at 4.5 in the forty-yard dash, and at the collegiate and professional levels he kept improving. At one point with the Jets he was clocked at 4.35. With each team he played on, he was among the fastest players. He kept finding another gear.

After Henry saw Bobby win the mile relay, he spoke with him about varsity football and the upcoming spring practice for the 1972 season. Bobby became excited about the future and began working out regularly in the weight room, building strength and endurance.

"That's the thing about Bobby," Henry said. "He had an incredible work ethic. He was not only the most talented athlete I ever coached, but he also exerted maximum effort to improve."

Spring football practice in 1972 lasted four weeks and ended with the jamboree at Hugh Mills Stadium among Albany High School and the city's other three public high schools. Bobby played free safety during the jamboree and showed great speed, and at one point ran across the field to tackle an opposing running back known for outstanding speed. Henry realized by the end of spring practice that Bobby was going to be special.

Summer came and Bobby ran and lifted weights, preparing himself for the notorious Graves Springs pre-season football camp. Many players dreaded it because of the extreme conditions of playing football in the woods. Players and coaches would meet at the high school on a Sunday afternoon and board buses to take them to camp.

The camp sat a half-mile or so off Graves Springs Road outside of Albany and in Lee County. There were three buildings on site. A wooden structure built in the 1930s served as B-team barracks. Players brought mattresses and laid them across wooden bunks. It had no plumbing, and players relieved themselves outside or in the creek. Players often opened the doors and urinated off the steps, until the smell of urine became so rancid that coaches put a stop to it.

Another wooden structure served as a cafeteria or "mess hall." And a cinderblock building providing sleeping quarters for both the varsity and coaches. It had showers and toilets, but most players, because the toilets were often stopped up, relieved themselves in the woods or the creek.

And most players did not shower but swam naked in the creek after each practice. The three daily practices were killers. Coaches did not give water breaks, even when the temperature approached a hundred degrees, and the first and third practice sessions lasted more than two hours each. The mid-day practice, for specialty teams, lasted about an hour.

Some players "fell out," as the expression went, because of dehydration and had to be carried off the field. When a player said, "Bear Got Him," he meant that one of his teammates during practice had gotten sick and left the field to vomit in the woods that surrounded the field. One player who became dehydrated and collapsed during the early 1970s was Brent Brock, who eventually became one of Bobby's teammates at FSU.

A practice field carved out of the piney woods was located about a hundred yards or so from the three buildings clustered together along the creek. Each morning coaches awakened players before daylight. Players dressed and walked to the cafeteria, and each took a salt tablet and a cup of orange juice. After that they walked slowly to the practice field and when it was light enough to see, coaches blew their whistles and the first practice began.

The first week in camp was for conditioning only, and players wore shorts, T-shirts, helmets, and cleats. The second week they were in full uniform, and during the first and third practices each day there were lots of drills and scrimmages in full contact. Wednesday night meant visitation, when girlfriends and family members were allowed at camp for a few hours.

After about the third or fourth day of camp, the field became more sand than grass, and players were irritated constantly by prickly sand spurs that dug into them when they fell to the ground. Once on the ground, red fire ants bit into them. Around the site and along the creek were thick oak, pine, and cypress trees, and the animals that lived in them. Players were only a few miles from home, but it seemed like a thousand.

Cooks from the high school cafeteria were bused out to camp each day to prepare the three daily meals. Eggs, pancakes, bacon, fried chicken, pork chops, mashed potatoes, and other dishes, as much as the players wanted, with ice cream in the evening. The team ate well.

A large tree along the Muckalee Creek had a rope tied to one of its branches and some players, not all, swung from the tree into the creek after each practice. Sixty naked football players swimming and playing in the creek after practice was not an uncommon sight. Upstream, players could see venomous cottonmouths or water moccasins sunbathing on the rocks in the middle of the creek. These dangerous snakes were sometimes aggressive. After three or four days of practice, some players walked naked upstream several yards on a dirt path and waded into the Muckalee Creek.

From there they would scare the snakes off the rocks, wade into mid-stream and beat their dirty uniforms on the rocks to clean them. Three-a-days in the same uniform saturated with sweat created an almost unbearable smell. There were no washing machines and dryers at camp. After several minutes of washing their filthy uniforms on rocks, they placed jock straps over their heads, covering one eye like an eighteenth century Caribbean pirate, and began their walk back to the barracks. They sang a song they made up for the occasion. *"Hey, hey, who are we! One-eyed pirates of the Muckalee! Hey, hey, who are we! One-eyed pirates of the Muckalee!"*

Once back into the barracks with wet uniforms, players hung them on their bunks and they were dried by the constant humming of electric fans.

After the final practice on the first Friday, players were bused back to the school and could spend Friday and Saturday at their homes, but they had to report back to school on Sunday to be bused again to Graves Springs, to begin the final week of camp. Camp was hard, some say cruel, and sometimes included midnight practices if players refused to stop talking when the coaches instructed them not to. Today the public outcry against such conditions for a high school football camp would be long and loud.

Graves Springs was designed to "make or break" a player, as a local sports writer wrote in the early 1960s, and it taught Bobby that shared hardship, camaraderie, and demanding coaches all helped forge a team. To make or break a player was understood by everyone who ever attended the camp over its fifty-year history.

Bobby flourished at camp. He became tougher both mentally and physically, which was what the camp intended to do. And for the first time in his life he lived and socialized daily with white boys.

At night Bobby and other black players talked and told stories with white players, teaching them the card game called Tonk. Black and white players played poker together as well. A dime would get a player in a poker game. They complained together about how tough camp was. They listened to music from eight-track tape players that included Led Zeppelin, Al Green, and the Spinners. They talked about girls, told dirty jokes, and shared *Playboy* and *Penthouse* magazines. The toughness of the camp, the demanding coaches, the ordeal of three-a-days, the no-water-during-practice rule, and the punishing heat bound the players together in shared experience. Both black and white.

With no air conditioning at camp, at night, when the lights were turned off, Bobby heard the rhythmic sound of the fans, and the crickets in the nearby woods. Sleep usually came soon and was precious. Exhausted bodies everywhere. Despite the harshness of Graves Springs, Bobby loved being there, being a part of something bigger than himself, and accepting the challenge of the football camp. His first year at Graves Springs, it was clear to Bobby he had found something he wanted to excel in.

"I felt like Graves Springs was the toughest camp I was ever associated with," Bobby said. "That includes the Jets. Graves Springs prepared me for FSU and the Jets. I wanted to be a part of Graves Springs. By the time we left camp to begin the season, we felt like we were a team."

Tackling and blocking drills at camp were stressed by the coaches, but often dreaded by the players. Coaches loved them. They were aimed to instill toughness in their players, to have players surpass their own perceived limitations.

One such killer-of-a-drill, "Root Hogging," involved two players, nose-to-nose on the field and in full uniform. Their teammates formed a circle around them. A coach blew his whistle and the two tried to run over one another, sometimes using their arms to club helmets.

"Rip his head off!" players shouted as the two attacked one another. This drill became intense and players hit and clawed, with fire in their eyes. They looked as if they wanted to kill one another. Coaches screamed during the drill for the players to fight until the end, until they were satisfied with the effort and then blew the whistle.

"There was lots of hitting at camp by the second week," Bobby said. "That was all part of the coaching philosophy back then. It was a way to make you tough."

Another favorite drill of the coaches, players referred to as "Beep, Beeps." During this drill a line of about ten players formed, and when a coach blew his whistle, the players sprinted down field as fast as they could. But the next time a whistle blew, after about ten or fifteen yards, players extended their arms birdlike and flew through the air, landing belly-first on the ground. After hitting the ground, players quickly got up and continued sprinting. At the sound of the next whistle, they belly-flopped again. During this drill, players hit the ground ten times, and if the coaches weren't satisfied with the effort, they would do it ten more times.

"A lot of what happened at Graves Springs was to make you mentally tough," Bobby said. "I know going to that camp in high school helped me compete in college and the pros."

Because of the three daily practices, no water to drink during practice, and the crushing heat, some players "fell out," or became weak and dehydrated and were unable to continue to practice. During Bobby's senior year at Graves Springs, 1973, a tenth-grader, Brent Brock, fell out about mid-way through the first week of camp. Coaches contacted his mother, who arrived at camp and took her son to see a doctor in Albany. Brent's body had grown weak at camp because he had eaten little food between practices. He drank a lot of water and Gatorade after each practice session and he had little appetite for food. Brent did return for the second and final week of camp and practiced every day.

Later Brent accepted a scholarship to FSU as an offensive lineman, joining Bobby in Tallahassee. After graduating from FSU, Brent coached high school football for several years in Georgia. Later he coached at Middle Tennessee State University.

"That situation put you in a position where you had to step forward and become a man," Brent said, describing Albany High's Graves Springs Football Camp.

During Bobby's senior year at camp he learned that sometimes coaches called four practices a day, instead of three. The last night at camp that year, coaches turned the lights off at ten as they usually did. Some players were restless and rowdy. Others just wanted to sleep. A group of players were talking loud and laughing.

"Some guys that night just didn't want to go to sleep," Bobby said.

More time went by and more talking and laughing. Then fruit and other pieces of food were thrown throughout the barracks. Finally someone hollered: *"You motherfuckers need to shut up! Shut up and go to sleep!"* Then there was a loud pop as something, a Coke bottle maybe, shattered after being thrown against a cinder-block wall.

"Man, we need to put our helmets on!" said Leonard Lawless, a junior fullback. He put on his helmet and snapped his chinstrap.

"Yeah, this shit's getting crazy," said Davey Davis, a junior offensive lineman. He put his helmet on, too.

Next to Davey's bunk, Donald Alley, another junior offensive lineman, placed a Styrofoam ice chest over his head for protection. But a thrown object tore through the ice chest. After that, Donald put his helmet on.

A few moments later, Coach Ferrell Henry entered the barracks and turned the light on. All the noise and commotion stopped.

"Y'all don't want to go to sleep," he said. "Then get your helmets, shoes, and shorts on. You got two minutes to be on the field. *Move it! Move it now!*"

Bobby and his teammates did as they were told. Henry, around midnight, told his assistant coaches to awaken the sophomores, who were assigned to another barracks, and get them on the field, too.

As players walked the hundred yards or so to the practice field with crickets chirping along the Muckalee Creek, coaches drove two pickup trucks toward the field. Henry instructed them to park the trucks at opposite ends of the field and keep the headlights on. The four beams of light provided Henry all he needed.

"I wasn't sure what we were going to do," Bobby said. "But I was sure Coach Henry was pissed."

"All right, all right let's have one line right here!" Henry said. *"Give me a line right here!"*

Several players formed a line and got into the three-point position across one of the end zones and prepared to run full speed for a hundred yards. The whistle blew and the first group of players took off and, as they did, they ran through sand, kicking up dust that filtered through the light beams of the pickup trucks.

"I bet y'all will go to sleep when we leave here," Henry said. "Give me another line! Right here! Right here!"

The second group of players lined up, awaiting the sound of the whistle. Like a giant snake weaving its way across the sand, as some parts are out front only to be overtaken by other sections of its slithering body, players pounded the sand while the stars were bright above them.

"How many of these things we gonna run?" a player asked Bobby.

"We'll run until Coach Henry says stop," Bobby said.

Coach Henry seemed to be in the mood to run the team until daybreak. "Line up! Line up! Keep runnin', keep runnin'!" he said.

After the players in their respective groups had run six or seven one hundred yard sprints, some began to tire and slowed down. This irritated Henry. "Boys you're slacking off on me," he said. "I'll make y'all run 'til the sun comes up if you stop hustling. You won't sleep at all tonight."

The team ran a few more sprints, just as hard as the first few. Legs were hurting. Everyone was breathing hard. Henry finally blew his whistle to call each player to gather around him.

"Now maybe y'all will go to sleep," Henry said.

He blew his whistle for the final time and pointed to the barracks. Returning to the barracks, Bobby and his teammates were quiet as they undressed and went back to bed. No more talking, laughing, or throwing objects around the barracks. They all knew that, soon, Coach Henry would awaken them for their morning practice.

"That was my last night at Graves Springs, and I'll never forget it," Bobby said. "Running those sprints at midnight was all part of the mental toughness the coaches were teaching us back then."

In 2014 I re-published a book I had written years earlier about the notorious high school football camp along the Muckalee Creek. With the re-publication of *Made or Broken: Football & Survival in the Georgia Woods*, I asked Bobby to write a new introduction for me. Below is some of what he wrote:

> . . . Going to Graves Springs was the very first time I had ever been away from home with complete strangers except for the few black players who also attended camp from my neighborhood – people like Johnny Coleman, Charles Kendrick, Clarence Isler, and Nathaniel Henderson, who would later be my college roommate at Florida State University, Emmanuel Wesley, and the aforementioned Charlie Johnson. We were a tight group, mainly from CME, an area located near Albany High, and didn't know any of the white players at all.
>
> After arriving at Graves Springs via a bus ride outside of the city limits in the woods, with snakes, sand spurs and a host of gnats as company, we settled in for the night. I was quite excited to be in this environment, but what I wasn't ready for were the hot, humid, unbearable three-times-a-day grueling practices in the woods, with no shade, no water, sand spurs and screaming coaches who seemed to enjoy torturing us. This was the closest thing to the military as I could imagine.

There were a lot of days I thought I would die from the heat, lack of water, up-down drills, sprints after practice, and on a midnight run because some players were too boisterous. But when I looked at players both black and white who pushed on, I drew strength from them. Jim Young and Bruce Shaw were two of the white players who provided leadership for us. Johnny "Mule" Coleman was an animal and an inspirational leader. I couldn't let them down.

The two years I spent at Graves Springs taught me valuable lessons that carried me throughout my life, even now: Through hard work, a unified effort, with a common goal, we all became equals! No matter our color. When we were on the field together between the white lines, we must love each other and fight for each other to have a chance to become champions, which we did.

It's the "bond of sports" that can overcome a lot of prejudices and preconceived notions better than any legislation that can be passed. Because of our time spent together, eating, laughing, crying, dreaming and fighting during camp, a mutual respect was established. All walls were knocked down, and new brothers were added to our families forever. Our children heard from us, their parents, that people should not be judged by the color of their skin but by the content of their character. We are a band of brothers today for the lessons learned at Graves Springs.

Several players who attended Graves Springs entered military service after high school, and for most of them the football training they endured was tougher than what the military demanded. At least the military gave them water breaks. There were a few other players from camp, like Bobby, who eventually played professionally, and in their experiences with other pre-season camps, none were tougher than Graves Springs.

Brad Oates, at six five and 215 pounds, graduated from Albany High in 1971, and accepted a scholarship from Brigham Young University, where he played defensive linemen. From

1976 to 1984 he played with a handful of NFL teams, including the Green Bay Packers.

"I was completely shocked by the conditions of Graves Springs," Oates said. "Frankly, after Graves Springs there wasn't anything in college or pro ball that I experienced that even came close. You never thought you were going to make it at camp. I remember as a player out there praying for little things, like practice to end early."

*

Leonard Lawless, a white player who moved to Albany from Iowa in the late 1960s when his father was transferred to a local Firestone plant, played at Graves Springs and Albany High for three years.

"We didn't have any racial problems out there because Henry and his staff weren't going to allow it," he said.

Leonard graduated from the University of Georgia and for years has worked as a certified public accountant in Albany. He said he admired and respected Bobby, not only for his ability and determination, but also for the decent and fair way he treated others.

During one scrimmage, Bobby was playing defense when Leonard took the handoff from the quarterback and broke through the line of scrimmage.

"I hit Bobby and he must have been off balance because he went down," Leonard said. "That just never never happened."

Leonard saw nothing but open field and the end zone. Leonard said he thought for certain he had a touchdown, but Bobby thought otherwise. Bobby got up from the ground and ran hard toward Leonard, catching him and tackling him before he scored. Leonard has never forgotten about that scrimmage and Bobby's determination.

Nathaniel Henderson, Bobby's boyhood friend and teammate at both Albany High and FSU, and other players under

Coach Ferrell Henry came to appreciate his high standards of discipline and fairness.

"What stands out to me was how fair he was with all his players," Henderson said. To Henderson and others, Henry became a father-figure and players could express themselves differently on the field as long as they worked hard and did their best. Henderson, who played defensive line, led through his actions, not by being vocal on the field like some of his teammates. Henry never looked at Henderson to be loud or like others.

Do your job on the field to your best ability. That's what mattered and that's what began to shape Bobby for his future as both a collegiate and NFL player.

Born in 1941 in rural Miller County, Georgia, about forty miles southwest of Albany, Henry came of age with few frills. His father, Jeff Henry, worked as a sharecropper, and the family lived in the country until Henry turned six. Then the family moved into Colquitt, the county seat.

Ferrell had one sibling, an older brother W. T. When they moved to Colquitt, Ferrell's father and mother, Ludie, found a number of menial jobs, including custodian work in various businesses.

"They had about every job nobody wanted," Ferrell said.

His father became a deputy sheriff for the county and his mother a school lunchroom worker. "Life was good but hard," Henry said. "When we started we started with zero" in terms of money.

Ferrell had been too young to help his father in the fields when he sharecropped. But as he and W. T. got older, they were hired by landowners to pick cotton by hand. For hours and hours under the hot sun, with backs bent and hands sometimes bleeding from the prickly plant, they filled up sacks with cotton. They earned three dollars for a hundred pounds picked.

With the money, their mother bought clothes for the upcoming school year.

One summer Jeff Henry bought a lawn mower for his sons, and they cut grass for homeowners throughout Colquitt. For each yard they cut, they could only keep fifty cents of what they earned. The rest of the money the family used to buy groceries or saved in a bank account and used for a down payment for cars the sons later purchased.

"There was never any doubt about going to college," Henry said.

Both boys earned athletic scholarships and graduate from college. W. T. played basketball at Troy State in Alabama, and Ferrell accepted a scholarship to play football at FSU after graduating from Miller County High School in 1959. Primarily a linebacker at six feet and 190 pounds, he played limited time on the offensive line.

After graduating, he was hired as an assistant football coach in 1964 by Harold Dean Cook at Albany High School. Cook had also grown up in Miller County, but the two did not know one another before Harold Dean hired Henry.

What Bobby Jackson came to learn from Ferrell Henry, self-discipline, hard work, and commitment to team, Henry himself learned from Harold Dean Cook.

"Harold Dean was one of the most disciplined men I had ever been around," Henry said. "He became my role model."

Harold Dean stressed fundamentals and hard-hitting practices. And so did Henry when he became head coach. In an age when many adults smoked, Harold Dean prohibited his coaches from smoking in front of his players.

During Henry's second year, 1965, as an assistant coach, the all-white team had its first black players. Two blacks arrived at Graves Springs Camp that year, Grady Caldwell and Ernest Jenkins. Ernest left the team during the first week of camp after being harassed by a group of white players.

Caldwell stayed, endured overt acts of racism, but ultimately accepted by the team and played two years before graduating and creating a pathway for other blacks like Bobby Jackson.

Caldwell's fascinating and inspiring life story includes political activism, years of drug addiction and incarceration, but later, redemption through God, as he became the senior pastor for New Mercy Baptist Church in Griffin, Georgia. Caldwell's life has been chronicled in a book he and I wrote, *To Dance with the Devil's Daughter: God's Restoration of the Rev. Grady Caldwell.*

Before white players accepted Caldwell as part of the team, Ferrell saw how Harold Dean did the "right thing" by supporting the team's lone black player during this volatile period of desegregation in the South, Henry said.

During one meal at camp, Caldwell sat at a table where a group of white players were eating. As he sat down, they in turn got up and moved to another table. Upon seeing this head coach Harold Dean Cook took a seat at the same table with Caldwell.

"There was never any doubt about how Harold Dean was going to handle integration," Ferrell said. "He was going to do the right thing. I don't even remember a whole lot of discussion about it."

There were other times during the 1965 season when Cook openly supported Caldwell. Once, when the team was traveling out of town, they stopped at a restaurant that refused to allow Caldwell to eat in the same dining area with his white teammates. In response, Cook refused service altogether and took his team to another restaurant where all his players could eat together.

"I admired Coach Cook," Caldwell said. "I knew the kind of pressure he was under from the white people in the community" not to allow a black player on the team.

Henry replaced Cook as head coach of Albany High School in 1970 and continued a pattern of fairness and toughness toward all players. And he led the team through the 1973 season, the end of Bobby's high school career, before leaving Albany High in 1974 to coach at nearby Crisp County High School.

Both Cook, who died 2010, and Henry viewed team as more important than race, and both in one sense defied the racism they had come of age in, growing up in South Georgia.

"White or black, it didn't matter," Henry said. "Our staff was going to give everyone an equal shot and do what's best for the team, and I think we did that during those years."

Part of Henry's staff included defensive back coach Ronnie Archer, a firebrand who demanded toughness from Bobby and others as he put them through drill after drill in preparation for Friday night games.

Henry hired Archer, who was coaching in Albany at Radium Springs Junior High School in 1970, and said he had been watching the way Archer coached and became impressed by what he saw. He wanted him at Albany High School. Archer did not disappoint.

If Henry and Archer saw an explosive hit on the practice field, they'd take their caps off and throw them on the ground and yell: "*Hot dang, boys, that's the difference between chicken salad and chicken shit!*" That was the extent of their profanity on the field.

Archer, an only child and born in 1945 in Tift County, Georgia, about forty miles east of Albany, had a determined competitive streak all his life. His father farmed and his mother worked as a cashier at Abraham Baldwin Agricultural College in Tifton, the county seat. He played basketball at Tift County High School and graduated in 1963. He then attended the two-year school, ABAC, and played for the school's basketball team. He later transferred to Georgia Southern College in

Statesboro, graduated there and accepted a job teaching and coaching at Albany Junior High School in 1967.

Later, he worked at Radium Springs Junior High and left there in 1970 to join Henry at Albany High. Along with becoming the team's defensive backfield coach, Archer became the head baseball coach at Albany High in the early 1970s. He brought enormous passion to both sports.

Henry spent more than thirty years in education, as teacher, coach, and administrator, before retiring in 1996. Then, in 2002, he ran for the Crisp County Commission, won, and served one six-year term. The attack on our country on September 11, 2001 influenced his decision to enter politics.

"I just wanted to give something back to the community," he said. "I wanted to help in any way that I could, to make things better for the future."

Archer left education and coaching for private business in 1974, the same year Henry accepted a coaching job at Crisp County, and Bobby's freshman year at FSU.

"Ronnie was just one helluva football coach," Ferrell said. "I tried to take him with me to Crisp County."

Archer taught Bobby, as a cornerback, to explode to the line of scrimmage and attack a running back. "Archer wasn't mean," Henry said, but aggressive every second, believed in hard work and demanded it from his players who, in the end, respected him.

Archer instilled into his defensive backs a desire to hit and win and play beyond their own perceived limitations. It's one of the valuable lessons athletic competition can offer. Watching Archer put his defensive backs through their fundamental drills became a show in itself.

"Hot-dang boys, when that running back turns the corner you gotta break down in a football position!" Archer said. "I mean keep your tail low!"

At this point during his instructions, Archer bent his knees, flex his arms out in front of his body, and clench his fists, all the while with his butt just inches from the ground, illustrating the proper football position to attack a running back.

"You've gotta hit and lock those arms! Keep drivin' your legs and tail and never let up. *Hot-dang, that's how it's done!*"

He said it this way many times over, and each time the excitement and enthusiasm overwhelmed him. This kind of desire spilled over into Bobby and stayed with him every time he stepped on a football field.

Bobby never let up going through drills at an Albany High football practice. He became one of "Archer's Boys." And when Bobby made a big hit in a drill or scrimmage, Archer responded.

"Boys, that's some lick!" Archer said. "Dang it, boys! That's what football's all about. Robert Jackson knows how to use that helmet!"

If the boys who played under Archer worked hard like Bobby they won his praise. He didn't tolerate players who didn't give everything they had on every play.

"Ronnie was the one who developed Robert Jackson," Henry said. "I remember the way Robert's eyes would light up" when Archer showed him how to hit, position his body correctly, or how to cover a wide receiver. "Robert learned everything he could from him."

Bobby has quoted Archer, who died in 2006, many times over the years: "It's not the size of the dog in the fight, it's the size of the fight in the dog."

To Bobby, both coaches stand out as instrumental figures who led to his success at the collegiate and professional levels.

"Coach Henry and Coach Archer molded me," Bobby said. "The other coaches, at FSU and the Jets, polished me."

CHAPTER 4

While Ferrell Henry and Ronnie Archer "molded" Bobby during his two years of varsity football, 1972 and '73, he played against not only some of the best teams in Georgia, but some of the best in the nation.

About ninety miles south of Albany were the Valdosta High School Wildcats. In 1971 they finished 13-0, including a 41-8 win over the Albany High School Indians and the State Championship in Region 1-AAA.

That same year, sports writers across the country proclaimed the Wildcats, coached by Wright Bazemore, to be the best high school team in the nation. Because of their many one-sided victories, sportswriters referred to the 1971 Valdosta team as one of the greatest in the history of high school football. Their average score was 48-12, and they won the state title by beating Avondale-Atlanta 62-12.

Bazemore's teams in 1962 and '69 were also recognized as the nation's best. Overall, Valdosta High has won six national championships, twenty-four state titles, and forty-two region titles. In 2008 ESPN named Valdosta - "Title Town."

Thomasville High, part of Albany High's schedule, were state champions in 1973, and again in '74 when they were selected America's best team. William Andrews played running back for Thomasville during this period and later, after playing at Auburn University, had an outstanding career with the Atlanta Falcons, where his number was retired. Bobby competed against Andrews at the high school level and again in the NFL.

"That region we played in was just so tough," Bobby said. "We faced some good teams back then. The caliber of play in high school helped me compete when I got to FSU."

Albany High School won a state title in 1959, the period before integration, and their best years after integration were 1966 and '67, when they won eight games each of those seasons. In 1971, they were 4-5-1.

As a junior, Bobby played free safety for the varsity in 1972. His cousin, Charlie Johnson, played in the defensive backfield as well.

"It was great being back there with Charlie," Bobby said. "We had been through a lot together as kids. Charlie was tough. He knew how to defend against the pass."

The team finished 6-4, but earned the title of City Champs against three other public schools: Monroe, Westover, and Dougherty. Against Dougherty, with Albany behind, Bobby fielded a punt around his own five-yard line, got two key blocks, one from Johnny "Mule" Coleman and the other from Nathaniel "Big Nate" Henderson, and scored the winning touchdown.

"I knew after that run he was going to be special," Johnny said. "That year he established himself as a hard hitter with a lot of key tackles."

He practiced and played with great intensity, always trying to get better. And that year he was selected as an All-Georgia High School defensive back. After football season ended, Bobby began training for track.

In the spring of 1973, Bobby ran a 40.7 seconds split, or quarter mile, as Albany High's mile relay team won first place in the region tournament in Fitzgerald while Bobby recorded his best time ever in the event. Bobby also finished first in the 440-yard-dash at the region meet, but did not run well later in that event during the state tournament in Atlanta, he said.

The relay team finished "fifth or sixth," Bobby said, disappointing him and others on that team at the state meet where Olympic gold medal sprinter Jesse Owens was Master of Ceremonies. "We weren't focused like we should've been," Bobby said. The relay team included Richard Wheeler, Theo Jacobs, and James Harpe.

A year behind Bobby, but a speedster himself, Harpe was an only child born in Ft. Gaines, Georgia, a small town on the Alabama-Georgia border. He also played football and looked to Bobby for leadership. His split at the region meet in Fitzgerald was 51.5 seconds.

James wore number 46 on his football jersey, Bobby wore number 45. And James said it was motivation for him to be close to Bobby's number. James played slot back his senior year, the same position Bobby played his senior year. All this mattered to James as he watched, learned from, and idolized Bobby Jackson.

"He was a role model for me," James said. "I wanted to emulate him. Plus Bobby got all the girls."

After graduating in 1975, James accepted a football scholarship at Springfield College in Massachusetts, played four years, and has remained in the state. He served in the Air National Guard for twenty years and, since the late 1980s, has worked for the state of Connecticut, including the state's judicial branch of court mediation for child protection.

For about twenty years, James has been involved in Brazilian Gracie Jujitsu. He earned a black belt and now owns a studio where he gives instruction. Physically, he remains solid and in excellent shape. James had seen plenty of hard-nosed hitters playing football in the 1970s in south Georgia, but none tougher than his teammate.

"The only way I can describe it was that everything was balled up and packaged," James said. "He was explosive and was fearless."

Bobby stood out on a team and in a region where there were many good football players, and his success in the NFL did not surprise his former high school teammate.

"Bobby was an outlier," James said. "He wasn't a normal athlete" because of the combination of speed, athletic ability, and desire to hit. "He was such a great high school athlete, but he was humble."

In high school, Bobby kept a modest Afro, dressed sharp, and kept above average grades, always mindful of his grandmother's expectations, and always appreciative of her support.

"I didn't want to disappoint her," Bobby said. "She had already laid a good foundation for me before I got to high school."

Bobby enjoyed the company of girls, and at one point dated Debra Coleman, a cheerleader. There were dances and parties where sometimes both blacks and whites socialized. At most of these events, alcohol was available and Bobby drank "a little" along with other teammates, he said.

"We had a lot of fun back then," Bobby said. "It was just a period where we got along with each other."

Off the field, students and teachers warmed quickly to Bobby, who carried an engaging demeanor and a smile on his face -- never boastful or arrogant about what he accomplished as an athlete.

During his senior season, Henry moved Bobby to slot back on a team that started with high expectations but finished 5-5. Bobby had an outstanding year and scored ten touchdowns. He caught a few touchdown passes from me as the team's quarterback. With his great speed, determination, and leaping ability, he became an easy target. Later, his vertical leap was measured at 32 inches.

One of his touchdowns in 1973 came from an 88-yard kickoff return against Crisp County High School. Bobby was picked as the team's top offensive player and selected to the All-Region and All-City teams after the season ended. Before the football year started, he began receiving letters of interest from colleges, including the University of Nebraska and Michigan State University.

Before he visited FSU, Bobby, Nathaniel Henderson, and their teammate Clarence Isler, a bruising fullback, were invited to visit the Iowa State campus. The three flew together and landed in the snow and bitter cold.

"The thing I remember about that trip was that it was just too cold for me out there," he said.

Of the three, Isler accepted a scholarship and played for Iowa State. Back in Georgia, FSU began pursuing Nathaniel Henderson.

Phil Spooner, Albany High's offensive backfield coach, who had played for the Seminoles, kept strong ties to the program in Tallahassee and urged the coaches there to sign Nathaniel and Bobby. Henry and Spooner drove Nathaniel and Bobby to Tallahassee to meet the FSU coaches and visit the campus.

"The coaches down there were a lot more excited about Nathaniel than Bobby," Henry said.

Big Nate, at six-foot five and around 245 pounds, had cancelled recruiting trips to both the University of Georgia and Notre Dame because of his growing interest in FSU. Some college coaches were concerned about Bobby's size, or lack of it, and there were few solid offers. He remained determined to play collegiate football somewhere.

"I had faith in Henry and Spooner," Nathaniel said. "I don't blame them for pushing FSU, that's where they played."

Besides, playing at FSU would keep Nathaniel closer to home and that became important to him, he said. "By me and Bobby going together, it helped with me making my decision."

Nathaniel, who had played defensive lineman at Albany High School, became an offensive line at FSU, where he earned a degree in criminology. The St. Louis Cardinals drafted Nathaniel but released him after one year. He then spent a year playing professional football in Canada before he left the game, beginning a career in the insurance business back in Georgia.

Convincing FSU to sign Bobby became more difficult than signing Nathaniel, Henry said.

"Bobby was just small, and I don't know if Bobby even knows this today," Henry said. "But FSU was not going to offer him a scholarship because of his size. They wanted Nathaniel Henderson and we said you got to take Bobby Jackson. They thought he was too small. He proved them all wrong."

Bobby and Nathaniel were not the only two Albany High players of that era that Henry had encouraged FSU coaches to sign. John Murphy graduated in 1970, after playing football when Henry was an assistant coach, and signed a scholarship with the Seminoles.

Murphy became one of the few blacks on the FSU team, the school having signed its first two black players in 1968, defying the all-white tradition. Murphy had an outstanding career at FSU, where he played linebacker, earned a degree, and returned to Albany to live and work. In 1965, Murphy joined a few other blacks by becoming the first to enroll at the all-white Albany Junior High.

Murphy came from nearby Lee County, just north of Albany, where his parents farmed for a living. Lee County, like many other areas of the South, experienced racial violence in the early 1960s.

Blacks there had been conducting civil rights meetings and voter registration drives in churches that were being fire-bombed by the Ku Klux Klan. Shady Grove Baptist Church had been burned to the ground. Homes of black families had been riddled with bullets by nightriders.

Murphy's parents moved the family to Albany to escape the racial violence in Lee County. Initially in Albany, he attended all-black Southside Junior High and academically he was one of the top students there. But by 1965, as he was entering the eighth grade, he chose to transfer to Albany Junior High to compete with white students in both sports and academics.

A few of Murphy's friends were critical of his decision to leave Southside. "I was ridiculed by some black folks for moving to Albany Junior High," Murphy said. "They thought I was trying to suck up to white folks. I just wanted to compete." Of those who were critical then, Murphy said, "I would say to them that you're not here at Albany Junior High because you're scared."

*

On December 9, 1973, Sunday, the *Albany Herald* published a picture of Bobby Jackson and Nathaniel Henderson signing athletic scholarships to play football at FSU. In the photo, both Nathaniel and Bobby are wearing their Albany High letter jackets and sitting at a table next to each other, with pens in their hands. Bobby's youthfulness, in two weeks he would turn just seventeen, was apparent in the photo.

Standing behind the two signees was Henry, Nathaniel's mother, Mrs. Jessie Henderson, Bobby's grandmother, Rebecca Jackson. The photo also includes Bobby's stepmother, Mrs. Laverne Jackson, who the paper identified as Bobby's mother.

Bobby's father did not attend the signing ceremony. Although Bobby and his father maintained a good relationship, his father often chose to stay away from the spotlight when it shone on his son.

"That was just the way he was," Bobby said. "I knew he was always there to support me. I always knew that."

Bobby got what he wanted, a football scholarship, and never once doubted his ability to play at that level. "All my life some people told me I was too small to play," Bobby said. "I knew better by the time I got to high school. I did prove some people wrong."

Confident going down to FSU, Bobby planned to work hard and be in the starting lineup as a freshman. It didn't take him long.

*

Prior to the 1972-73 academic school year, the NCAA prohibited freshmen from playing on varsity football and basketball teams. In 1968, rules were changed to allow freshmen to play in all other sports except football and basketball. One of the worst tragedies in American sports history led to the NCAA changing its freshmen eligibility rules for those two sports in 1972.

On November 14, 1970, a chartered jet carrying most of the Marshall University football team crashed into a hillside near Kenova, West Virginia. All seventy-five people on board were killed, including thirty-seven football players and eight coaches. The team was returning home to Huntington, West Virginia, after a 17-14 loss to East Carolina University. As a result of the crash, the NCAA allowed Marshall to play freshmen in 1971, then applied the ruling to every school the following year.

Both Bobby and Nathaniel had earned enough credits to graduate early, December 1973, from Albany High School. By January they were roommates and enrolled at FSU. They participated in spring practice in preparation for the upcoming season. Back in Albany, Henry took bets with his fellow coaches and others who knew Bobby when he would earn a starting position.

"If I'm not mistaken, Bobby didn't start the first game as a freshman," Henry said. "Then he went in after one of his teammates was injured. He started every game after that."

Bobby actually started the first game of his freshman season against Pittsburgh University and had an interception. For the rest of that year and the next three, he started for FSU.

This didn't surprise Henry and others who watched Bobby play at Albany High School. *It's not the size of the dog in the fight, it's the size of the fight in the dog.*

"I think the greatest surprise was that he didn't get injured, not enough to miss a game," Henry said. "He worked hard at practice down there and in the weight room. I think he had to do everything he could to compensate for his size. Signing Bobby Jackson was a steal for their program."

Since his high school days Bobby has remained close to Henry and his wife, Arleeta. The Henry's traveled to Tallahassee often after Nathaniel and Bobby were signed, watching the two play, and visiting with them after the games.

Throughout Bobby's career with the Jets, he often called Henry, updating him on his life and career. The Henry's never saw Bobby play in person at the professional level, but followed his games on television. Bobby once gave Mrs. Henry a picture of himself in his Jets' uniform and signed, "To Momma Arleeta."

"Bobby was just always so kind and respectful," Mrs. Henry said. "I think Ferrell in some ways was a surrogate father to him. I was always impressed by the way he cared for his grandmother."

Bobby, after he became a professional football player, bought a house for his grandmother, Rebecca Jackson, in Albany.

Henry remains today one of the most important men in Bobby's life. "I couldn't have had the success I had without him," Bobby said. "When Nathaniel and I went to FSU, he was there supporting us. I'll always appreciate what he did for me. Plus, he helped a lot of young players over the years."

*

Like many American boys in the early 1970s, Bobby was captivated by the growing popularity of the NFL and the nationally broadcast games on television. He'd sit for hours during the weekends watching both collegiate and professional games on a black-and-white television.

These games fueled his drive to succeed on the football field and defy those who said he was too small to be a great player.

"I became fascinated watching games back then, and my favorite college team was Ohio State," Bobby said. "I watched Jack Tatum on defense, and he played monster man. That was a cross between a safety and linebacker. And, man, he hit like a monster! That's how I wanted to play. That's how I did play. I patterned my game after Jack Tatum."

Tatum played ten years in the NFL and most of that was with the Oakland Raiders. He was selected to the Pro Bowl three times. Tatum's hits were described as brutal and violent. "I like to believe my best hits border on felonious assault," he said.

During a pre-season game in 1978, Tatum's hit left New England Patriot wide receiver Darryl Stingley paralyzed. Tatum published a book in 1980 called, They Call Me Assassin. In it he wrote, "When the reality of Stingley's injury hit me with its full impact, I was shattered. To think that my tackle broke another man's neck and killed his future." Stingley died in 2007 at the age of 55.

During the 1980 season, when Tatum played for the Houston Oilers, the Jets beat the Oilers at Shea Stadium. After the game Bobby took his copy of Tatum's book to the Oilers' locker room.

"I took the fastest shower in NFL history, so I could race across to their locker room and wait to get Jack Tatum's autograph," Bobby said. "I was like a little kid, waiting outside with other autograph seekers and members of Tatum's family." Tatum died of a heart attack in 2010 at the age of 61.

Bobby also found an inspirational player on Ohio State's offense during the early 1970s. Running back Archie Griffin was about Bobby's size and he wore number 45, Bobby's high school number. Griffin became the only player in college history to win the Heisman Trophy twice, in 1974 and '75, his junior and senior years. What Griffin had on his helmet influenced what Bobby put on his when he played high school and college ball.

"He had all those Buckeyes on his helmet for big plays and I put decals on mine at Albany High just like Griffin did," Bobby said. "When I got to FSU, I put tomahawks on my helmet for big plays. We were about the same size and we both started in college as freshmen. He was my soulmate, and I had his picture inside my locker at FSU. I wanted to emulate Griffin back then."

For his career at Ohio State, Griffin rushed for 5,589 yards and 26 touchdowns. He was drafted in the first round in 1976 by the Cincinnati Bengals and played there for seven seasons. Throughout his NFL career he rushed for 2,808 yards and seven touchdowns.

From the Midwest to the Pacific coast, Bobby followed players who, whether they knew it or not, guided his career. In 1972, when Bobby was a junior in high school, he watched on television a game between the University of Southern California and Notre Dame. And he watched closely USC running back Anthony Davis, known as "A. D."

"It was the greatest game I recall seeing in my life," Bobby said. "It was one of those back-and-forth games. Davis scored six touchdowns. It was the greatest performance on a football field I had ever seen."

Davis took the opening kickoff 97 yards for a touchdown in the USC 45-23 victory. Later, Davis returned another kickoff 96 yards for a touchdown. During his career at USC, Davis scored 11 touchdowns in three games against Notre Dame. He was called the "Notre Dame Killer."

Again, Bobby drew inspiration from a player about his size. And a player with exceptional speed.

"I related to Davis and he gave me hope," Bobby said. "After watching that game with Davis, I began to think, 'Why can't I do that? I got what they got, just gotta do it. I got the dream.' "

While Davis was runner-up for the 1974 Heisman Trophy, his professional career did not match what he did in college. He had a disappointing and injury-plagued pro football career that included stints in the now-defunct World Football and United Football Leagues, as well as in the Canadian Football League and the NFL. But he remains one of Bobby's early models.

A few years before Bobby played at Albany High School, cornerback Larry West excited its fans with his brilliant speed and overall athleticism. West graduated from Albany High in 1971, Bobby's sophomore year, and he was one of the first black players given a full scholarship to the University of Georgia and signed by head coach Vince Dooley. Bobby watched West play high school ball and watched how he trained.

"I used to watch Larry running stadium steps in our stadium on hot Georgia afternoons," Bobby said. "He ran sprints and lifted weights in the weight room underneath our stadium."

Influenced by West, when Bobby got to high school he asked Coach Henry to give him a key to the weight room so he could access it anytime he wanted. Henry agreed.

"I just emulated Larry and got a key to the weight room," Bobby said. "That's how success is created – putting in the work."

West graduated from UGA and years later became a Baptist minister living with his family in Washington D. C. His aunt,

McCree Harris, was a pivotal leader in the push for civil rights in Albany. She encouraged West and a few other top black athletes to attend Albany High School in the late 1960s, join the football team, and help shatter racial barriers in the city.

On September 11, 1976, Bobby watched on television UGA play the University of California at Berkley in Athens. Cal had a wide receiver, Wesley Walker, who wore number 99. That day Walker had more than over 200 yards in receptions, Bobby said, as the Bulldogs won 36-24. Walker later had an outstanding career with the New York Jets and became one of the top receivers in the NFL by the late 1970s and early '80s.

"Wesley ended up being one of my teammates with the Jets and one of my best friends in life," Bobby said. "I'll never forget watching him in Athens that day. He torched the Bulldogs."

*

Bobby said he's thankful to many, both players and coaches, who inspired, motivated, and helped him along the way. But he had the dream and worked to fulfill it. This book is dedicated to his Albany High School coaches because they helped Bobby fulfill his dream, he said.

"I humbled myself and took their instruction on faith and did the work," Bobby said. "That's one of the secrets of success. I accepted that Coach Henry and Coach Archer and the others knew more than I did, and I wanted their knowledge. Some great players at all levels helped me. I couldn't have done this alone. There are too many to mention, but I did mention a few."

It takes many to fulfill a man's dream.

CHAPTER 5

Bobby arrived at FSU with the football program in disarray. The team was 0-11 in 1973 and several players had left the program because of what newspapers described as "low morale" and lack of financial support from the school's administration.

Newspaper stories in Florida over the following summer reported that FSU coaches lacked adequate training facilities, but they had put players through harsh and even dangerous training conditioning. One example was an off-season training technique that used chicken wire to keep players in crouched positions during their drills.

Head Coach Larry Bruce Jones complied a 15-19 record for three consecutive seasons beginning in 1971. He had played both linebacker and center at Louisiana State University, and had been an assistant coach there, and for a few other schools, before FSU hired him for the 1971 season. After the dismal 1973 season, school officials replaced Jones with Darrell Mudra for the 1974 season.

From 1969-73, Mudra was the head coach at Western Illinois University, where he compiled an overall 39-13 record. Mudra's offensive coordinator, Dan Henning, recruited Bobby to play wide receiver. The opportunity to continue to play offense after an outstanding senior year in high school excited Bobby, he said. But Henning's plan would be subverted by his fellow coaches. Henning later coach for the Jets, and he became head coach for the Atlanta Falcons, where Bobby played his final year.

In the spring of 1974, as Bobby and the Seminoles were practicing for the upcoming season, Henning missed a few practice sessions because of recruitment trips outside of Tallahassee. During his absence, the defensive coaches told Bobby to cover wide receivers during passing drills, and they were impressed with what they saw.

His speed, overall athleticism, and dogged coverage stood out. Bobby hit upperclassmen hard after they received the ball. Coaches liked what they saw and convinced Mudra to move Bobby from offense to defense. He accepted this without complaint, because he wanted a starting position and worked hard to get one. Donald "Deek" Pollard, the FSU defensive back coach, lobbied hard to have Bobby play defense.

Henning had plans for Bobby catching passes and scoring touchdowns, but those ended once he returned from the recruiting trip and became aware of the change.

"I wanted Bobby as a wide receiver, but Deek stole him from me," Henning said. "The rest is history."

Pollard, born in 1939 in Roodhouse, Illinois, attended Western Illinois University and played cornerback from 1957 through '61. After graduating, he became head football coach for Pittsfield High School in Illinois, where he complied an incredible 55-4-3 record, including fifty-four consecutive wins. Leaving the high school game, he took a job as an assistant coach at Western Illinois before coming to FSU in 1974.

He only coached at FSU for two years before leaving the school to coach at Oklahoma State University. Pollard spent about forty years coaching at the collegiate and professional levels, including teams such as the New York Giants and the Cleveland Browns. When Bobby arrived at spring practice in 1974, he made an impression on Pollard, not only as a player.

"When Bobby came to Tallahassee," Pollard said, "as a second semester senior in high school, he looked a lot like an undernourished seventh-grader."

Pollard called Bobby "Bojack," a nickname that stuck. Once spring practice had begun, Pollard thought less about Bobby's size and more about what he could do on a football field.

"Bobby was extraordinarily talented," Pollard said. "He had unbelievable feet, unbelievable quickness, and unbelievable ball skills," in terms of catching the football. "Henning wanted him on offense, but I wasn't going to let that happen."

Pollard said in 2015, from his home in Scottsdale, Arizona, that he has seen many football players during his long coaching tenure, but few with the blend of athleticism, determination, and work ethic Bobby displayed at FSU. Other things about Bobby he recalled from his FSU days.

"About the only thing better than his athletic ability was his character," Pollard said. "He was very quiet and an unassuming guy. He was coachable, and he was one of the finest young men I ever worked with."

During Pollard's two-year stay at FSU, the starting defensive backfield, along with Bobby, included other outstanding players who also played in the NFL. One was Lee Nelson from Melbourne, Florida, who had played at Pensacola Junior College. FSU did not offer Nelson a scholarship in 1974, but he joined the team and earned one.

Nelson also earned a starting position that year and led the team with eighty-six tackles. After his senior year his teammates selected him as the team's most valuable defensive player, and the St. Louis Cardinals drafted him in the fifteenth round. He played ten seasons in the secondary for the Cardinals and on kickoff and return teams. Like Bobby, he had a deserved reputation as a hard hitter.

"I don't know if it was the best secondary FSU ever had," Pollard said. "But it was one of the most talented ones." After coaching Bobby for two seasons, Pollard left the school. He followed closely the remainder of Bobby's collegiate career and his years in the NFL.

"To start four years at FSU and eight years for the Jets," Pollard said, "is almost unheard of. There's no question he was one of the top corners in the NFL for several years."

Bobby had a great spring at FSU in 1974, showing outstanding coverage against all the receivers he was matched against during practice sessions. Bobby said he felt confident from the beginning. He knew he had to prove himself, because players and coaches would judge him as someone who couldn't compete in major college football.

He worked hard and earned their respect. Pollard's tough and demanding coaching-style reminded Bobby of Ronnie Archer, his defensive backfield coach at Albany High. Both coaches were meticulous in terms of teaching defensive techniques, and both expected supreme effort from their players on every play. Both loved to see their players hit with fury. That's the way Bobby played. He made a quick impression on Pollard, as he had on Archer.

One day during spring practice in full pads, Bobby defended upcoming senior receiver Joe Goldsmith, who couldn't get open for the pass. Goldsmith became frustrated and a fight broke out between him and Bobby. Coaches allowed them to fight a few minutes before they stopped it. Lots of punches were thrown, but neither player was hurt. Bobby made a statement about his toughness on the field, something he would do time after time.

Leon Bright, from Merritt Island High School in Merritt Island, Florida, came to FSU the same year Bobby did and was an outstanding running back for the Seminoles. Bright rushed for 675 yards during the 1975 season at FSU, but only played two years before signing a professional contract. In high school he rushed for 4,036 yards while scoring seventy-seven touchdowns. He was later named to the Florida High School All-Century Team as one of the greatest of players in state history.

After leaving FSU, Leon had a fine career with the British Columbia Lions of the Canadian Football League, and he later joined the NFL, playing for the New York Giants and then the Tampa Bay Buccaneers. In 1982 while with the Giants, he led the league in punt returns with an 8.8-yard average. These two young players became part of a rebuilding process for FSU. Bright soon learned about the competitiveness of his new teammate.

"Both of us were skinny kids coming to FSU," Leon said. "Bobby was one of those guys who hated to lose at anything. He was going to out-do everybody, and he had a little temper."

During one practice a group of NFL scouts came to evaluate some of the players, but it was a time when there were few seniors on the team. The three fastest on the team were Bobby, Leon, and Nathaniel "Nat" Terry from Tampa, Florida. Like Bobby and Leon, Nat, a defensive back, was a freshman in 1974.

All three could run the forty-yard-dash around 4.35 seconds. Nat was drafted by the Pittsburgh Steelers in 1978, played six games and was released. Then the Detroit Lions signed him. While playing with the Lions that year, he returned a kickoff and chipped a vertebra in his neck, ending his professional career.

That day during their FSU practice, the scouts asked the three speedsters to race. They needed no further encouragement.

"When we lined up I let Bobby put me between him and Nat," Leon said. "I never should've done that. When the race started it was close, but in the end they squeezed me out and Bobby won. Bobby could fly. He just didn't know how fast he was."

If a player in a drill or scrimmage got the best of Bobby at practice, he'd make sure there'd be retribution before the practice ended.

"All that friendship stuff you got to lay aside during practice," Leon said. "But Bobby and I became friends and did things together away from the field."

Leon played against some outstanding football players in high school, as Bobby had, and had seen some hard hitters. Leon watched Bobby many times, during scrimmages and games, put explosive hits on receivers, telling them not to come to his side of the field. Bobby didn't let up. Not once.

Leon became concerned for Bobby's own safety and told him he was going to hurt himself if he kept hitting people in such a manner.

"Man, this is football," Bobby said. "Take no prisoners."

Bobby played that way in high school, and he was going to do the same in college. He never considered playing any other way.

"He hit about as hard as anyone I'd ever seen," Leon said.

During one game his freshman year, Bobby suffered a crushing tackle and had to be helped off the field. FSU, 1-10 that year, played close some highly ranked teams, including the University of Alabama that finished number one in the nation. FSU played Alabama October 12, 1974, in Tuscaloosa. Noise from the home-fans pulsated throughout the game.

Under Coach Paul "Bear" Bryant, Alabama had won the national championship the previous year, being led by one of the greatest college coaches ever.

Along with Bobby, there were a handful of other true freshmen that started for FSU. At one point during the game, Bobby and Leon were in position to field a punt, both starting in the defensive backfield. Bobby had earned at least one nickname during his first season.

"Bobby had had a sensational game," Leon said. "We called him the 'Shut-Down Corner.' "

As the ball sailed high overhead with thousands of cheering Alabama fans, Leon decided not to field the punt because of the ball's high hang-time and encroaching Alabama players.

Let the ball hit the ground, stay away from it, and hope for the best field position for their offense. The defenders would be too close to them by the time the ball was catchable, therefore they wouldn't be able to advance the ball up field, Leon said. Plus, if they did field it, they'd be hit immediately and risked a fumble. The fifty-eight thousand plus fans had seen a number of hard hits that day and were about to see another.

Leon told Bobby not to catch the ball. He yelled it over and over. Bobby's eyes remained focused on the ball as he positioned his body under it, arms and hands at the ready.

"I told him not to catch it," Leon said. "The crowd was so loud Bobby never heard me. *Man*, he got crushed right after he caught it."

Bobby received a monstrous hit, but he held on to the ball as he fell to the ground with the tackler on top of him. After the hit he could not get up on his own, and the officials called time-out.

Bobby's teammates helped him off the field and to the locker room to be examined by a team physician, who found no immediate or serious injuries.

"When they woke me up in the locker room," Bobby said, "I was still holding the ball. I wouldn't let go of it."

Because of the noise from the fans, Bobby did not hear Leon telling him to stay away from the ball. He did return to the game after that hit, and Alabama won 8-7 after scoring twice in the last eighty-seven seconds of the game. FSU fans, Bobby's teammates and coaches, and opposing players came to realize the toughness of the young cornerback from Albany, Georgia. The same one whose junior high coaches said was too small to play.

During his freshman year, Bobby had two interceptions, including one in the opening game at home against Pittsburgh University on September 14, when the Seminoles loss 6-9. His second interception came at Auburn during a 6-38 loss on October 26. He led the team that year in punt returns with 182 total yards for ten returns and one touchdown.

The lone touchdown came in Tallahassee on November 16 during 21-56 loss against Virginia Tech, when Bobby dazzled the home crowd with an 80-yard run to the end zone. The only victory for the Seminoles that year, 21-14, was over the University of Miami the week before the Virginia Tech game.

Bobby established himself as a leader, tough hitter, and an outstanding punt returner on a team that, by the time he finished his senior year in 1977, transformed itself into a national powerhouse.

CHAPTER 6

Earl Humes played defensive back at Miami Beach High School in south Florida before the Seminoles signed him in 1972, two years before Bobby arrived at FSU. Growing up, Humes turned early and often to God for guidance.

During the first game of one season in high school, his football team was losing at half time, and the coach asked Earl to lead the team in prayer.

"We had black kids and Jewish kids," Earl said. "It was a pretty good mix." Earl called his team together to pray, and they went on to win the game.

Earl still follows God's Word as an ordained Baptist minister, and for several years has lived in Orangeburg, South Carolina, where he has worked as an area director for the Fellowship of Christian Athletes. When Bobby arrived at FSU, Earl not only befriended him, but became a mentor to him.

"My first memory of Bobby was that he had graduated early from high school," Earl said. "When I saw him, he was just this baby-faced kid who looked like he should've been in the tenth or eleventh grade."

After watching Bobby at a few team practices, Earl thought less about Bobby's youthful appearance and more about something else: the explosive way he hit ball carriers and his excellent pass coverage.

"It wasn't long before I knew this kid was special. He was extremely gifted. The other thing I learned later was that he was humble. He didn't get the big head."

When Earl arrived at FSU, defensive back James "J. T." Thomas reached out to mentor Earl and help him adjust to college life, both on and off the field. Thomas, a native of Macon, Georgia, became one of the first blacks to start on an FSU football team. Thomas played safety his final year, earning All-American honors.

Being one of the few blacks on the team himself, Earl learned how to properly carry himself, respecting himself and others, from watching and emulating Thomas. In 1973, the Pittsburgh Steelers drafted Thomas in the first round, and he played for the team until 1981, winning four Super Bowls along the way. He became a key part of the Steelers' dominant defense of that period. Thomas became the first black person to letter in football at FSU, and the first black player to earn a degree there.

"J. T. had been a mentor to me," Earl said. "I wanted to return that and help someone else. That someone else was Bobby."

Bobby and Earl became close, with Earl at times watching over him and ensuring that he remained humble.

J. T. Thomas has sometimes been mistakenly referred to as the first black person to accept a football scholarship at FSU. In 1968, Coach Bill Peterson recruited the school's first two black players and offered them scholarships.

A few years earlier, FSU had enrolled the school's first non-athlete black students, as other schools throughout the South were doing during the nation's Civil Rights Movement. Ending the all-white tradition on the FSU football team in 1968 was running back Calvin Patterson from Miami and fullback Ernest Cook from Daytona Beach. Patterson had been one of the first blacks to play for Palmetto High School in Miami.

Once the two black players accepted the offers, they begin to receive hate mail full of racist threats. The letters were direct physical threats to Patterson and Cook. Their family members became worried about what might happen to them if they attended FSU and played football there.

Cook decided, in the end, not to enroll at FSU and eventually played for the University of Minnesota, where he attended medical school. He became a family-care physician. But Patterson enrolled at FSU. He became part of the team, but never played a varsity down.

Patterson struggled academically, lost his eligibility for a period, and suffered emotional problems while at FSU. On August 16, 1972, the day before the Seminoles were to start practice his senior year, Patterson shot and killed himself with a .38 revolver.

While Patterson's story is tragic, he courageously began the tradition that led to many outstanding black football players, like Bobby, enrolling at FSU.

*

Earl Humes convinced Bobby to join the Alpha Phi Alpha fraternity at FSU, and he began to participate in other aspects of college life, not just football. Bobby went to parties and enjoyed the company of girls, while Earl encouraged him to temper his off-field behavior.

"I always prayed for Bobby to stay away from all the temptations," Earl said. "We were all raised as children of God, and I knew he had a lot of talent and I didn't want to see him waste it."

Earl tried to influence Bobby, not so much by talking to him, but by showing him *how* to live. Earl's influence over Bobby during this period is one reason that Bobby, when he became a professional athlete living in New York, began regularly speaking to young people about the dangers of alcohol and drugs and the importance of taking care of their minds and bodies.

"Earl helped me keep my head straight when I was at FSU," Bobby said. "I've always appreciated what he did for me. I tried to help others like Earl helped me."

*

Bobby spent time with girls in Tallahassee while dating Saundra Litman, who lived in Albany. Saundra became pregnant with Bobby's child. Bobby, a few years older than Saundra, met her when she attended junior high school.

Born in 1959 in Tifton, Georgia, about an hour's drive east of Albany, Saundra came from a close-knit family. At round four or five, her family moved to Albany where her father, Bishop J. L. Litman, pastored a church called House of God Saints in Christ located on Whitney Avenue. That part of Albany became a central meeting place for activists involved in the Civil Rights Movement of the early 1960s.

By 1973, Saundra was a sophomore at Albany High, and the couple began dating. They went to movies together and once Bobby travelled with Saundra's family two hours east from Albany to hear her father preach at a church in Douglas, Georgia.

"We had fun together," Saundra said. "He was attractive. He was attracted to me. I just liked him as a person."

When Saundra learned she was pregnant in 1975, she told her parents and that she and Bobby planned to get married. The out-of-wedlock pregnancy caused tension in the Litman family.

"My parents didn't take it very well," Saundra said. "I was the apple of my father's eye. He had greater expectations for me."

The couple married in 1975 in the Litman's backyard on Newton Road in Albany, with one of her father's junior ministers performing the small ceremony attended by members of both families.

Both Bobby's grandmother and father supported his decision to marry Saundra, he said. At one point before the ceremony, Saundra's father told Bobby that he had a gun in his pants pocket to ensure that Bobby did the right thing and married his daughter.

"He laughed a little when he told me about the gun," Bobby said. "I didn't know if he was telling me the truth or not. It wasn't a good situation."

A few months after the ceremony, their child Indya was born on September 5, 1975. The couple and their child eventually moved into the married housing complex on the FSU campus. Soon there were problems in the marriage, and they divorced a couple of years later.

"It was hard when we were married," Saundra said. "I wanted to be in college just like he was, but I couldn't. We were very young. He wasn't settled-minded, and I wasn't either."

After the divorce, Bobby provided limited financial help to Indya while he remained in college, but more after he signed a contract with the Jets. He spent regular time with his young daughter, until leaving for New York in 1978.

"He did take up time with Indya before going to the NFL," Saundra said. "I do remember him doing that."

Bobby said he had been unemotionally ready for marriage, but because Saundra had become pregnant, the right thing to do was marry her. "Saundra was a wonderful person," he said. "I just didn't love her like a husband should love his wife."

Today Saundra, who remarried, lives in Tallahassee, and said she and Bobby remain friends. Indya became the first of Bobby's seven children born to four different mothers.

"My grandmother kept such a tight rein on me, when I got out there," Bobby said. "I got out there."

*

During the 1975 season the Seminoles improved, going 3-8, and Bobby, again a leader on defense, had five interceptions and led the team in punt return yardage. On November 1 at Clemson, Bobby had two interceptions as FSU won 43-7. FSU lost some close games that year, including Iowa State 6-10, Auburn 14-17, Memphis State 14-17, and Miami 22-24.

"We were in a lot of those games my first two years at FSU," Bobby said. "There was a lot of talent on that team, and I just thought then if we kept working, we'd get better. We lost a lot of close games my first two years there."

Before Bobby began his junior season, FSU made a coaching change that ultimately lead to a national football powerhouse in Tallahassee.

FSU fired Darrell Mudra over what newspapers had reported as "discontentment among fans and alumni" because of four wins in two years. The school hired Bobby Bowden to replace him. Bowden had been the head coach at West Virginia University from 1970-75 and compiled a 42-26 record there. Bobby, as well as the rest of the team, soon noticed things were going to be different after Bowden arrived. Things were going to be better, too.

During the games Mudra was in the press box and not on the field with his team. He gave his assistants probably more authority than most other coaches during that period, Bobby said.

After leaving FSU, Mudra became head coach at Eastern Illinois University, where he won the I-AA national championship in 1978. He finished his career as head coach for Northern Iowa University in 1987. His overall coaching record was 200-81-4 and in 2000 he was inducted into College Football Hall Fame as a coach. His nickname was "Dr. Victory," but it did not fit his short tenure at FSU.

Bowden came to Tallahassee with a coaching style that reminded Bobby of his high school coach in Albany, Ferrell Henry. Bobby called Bowden an "old fashioned" coach in terms of discipline and authority. Bowden did not sit in the press box during games.

Bowden stressed respect for yourself, your teammates, and your family, Bobby said. Bobby and his teammates were both impressed and hopeful with the coaching change. But not long after Bowden arrived, Bobby and other black players developed concerns about their new coach.

Mudra, a native of Omaha, Nebraska, had set a tone of fairness toward all players, white or black, when competing for positions. "Mudra always had these little philosophical viewpoints that he shared with the team," somewhat unorthodox compared to other coaches, "but that was just his style," Bobby said.

He allowed players to express themselves by wearing their hair long, and for Bobby and other blacks that meant full Afros. Bowden quickly changed this. Bowden didn't allow facial hair or long hair and made players adjust accordingly. Bobby and other black players who kept full Afros had to abide by the new coach and new rules but at first believed they were being discriminated against by a "southern white guy," Bobby said.

Bowden was born in 1929 in Birmingham, Alabama, a city where whites in the 1960s and decades before perpetuated many acts of violence against blacks. In Birmingham, there had been some of the worst acts of racial discrimination in our country's history. While at first concerned about Bowden and his fairness toward black players, Bobby and his black teammates came to realize that he wasn't "picking" on them and that all players, black or white, would be treated fairly.

"Myself and other black players had some biases of our own we had to overcome," Bobby said.

Not long after Bowden accepted the job at FSU, new facilities were built to support the football program. Bowden told his team to respect the new buildings and the money being spent on them. At one point, Bowden said they had better appreciate and take good care of these new facilities, and that in some cases they were better than the homes some of his players had grown up in. Bobby, like some of his teammates, grew up in public housing.

"Some of us came from the projects, and at first we didn't like what he was saying," Bobby said. "But the more we thought about it, we realized he was right. He was just giving us a lesson in respect."

Respect came to be one of the most important lessons Bowden taught. He reinforced what Bobby had learned from his coaches back at Albany High School.

"You knew who was in charge, and it was Coach Bowden," Bobby said. "He didn't cuss. He did it the right way. He reminded me of Coach Henry because they were both men who cared about their players. Both taught me things about life that helped me beyond football."

*

During Bowden's first year, 1976, the team finished 5-6. FSU lost their first three games then posted two consecutive wins. On October 2, they were at home against Kansas State and won 20-10. The following week, away at Boston College, they won 28-9. The other victories that year were the final three games of the season. They beat Southern Mississippi 30-27, as FSU quarterback Jimmy Black completed 21 of 39 passes for 351 yards and two touchdowns.

Then they beat North Texas State 21-20. FSU's final game that year was against Virginia Tech, and the Seminoles won 28-21 at home as running back Larry Key rushed thirteen times for 154 yards and one touchdown.

"Coach Bowden set the tone that year," Bobby said. "We had the talent and good players coming in the program. I was looking forward to my senior year."

During his senior year, the team's most successful one while Bobby played, Larry Key became the first FSU player to rush for more than 1,000 yards. He finished the 1977 season with 1,117 yards and a career-total of 2,953 yards. Bobby Butler, out of Atlantic High School in Delray Beach, Florida, joined FSU that year and played in the defensive backfield.

Bobby Butler, like Bobby Jackson, had an outstanding career at FSU and played in the NFL. Drafter by the Atlanta Falcons in 1981, Butler played twelve seasons for the team.

*

Bobby Jackson pulled a hamstring during the 1977 season and took karate lessons to improve his flexibility. He had been fortunate and almost injury-free at FSU, missing only one game during his four-year career. His off-season workouts were intense, the same as they had been at Albany High, in terms of weight lifting and running. A lot of hard work, excitement, and anticipation marked the Seminoles' pre-season camp in '77, Bobby Jackson said.

"I remember a lot of guys at camp confident we were going to do well that year," Bobby said. "By then we had the talent and the coaching. And we were fired up about what we could accomplish."

FSU opened away against Southern Mississippi and won 35-6. The following week Bobby had an interception at Kansas State, again another Seminole victory, 18-10. His second interception that year came at home on October 8, during a 14-0 win over Cincinnati. In that same game, he had a 54-yard punt return.

The Seminoles had only two regular season losses in '77. The first came at home on September 24 against Miami, 17-23. On November 19, they lost 16-41 at San Diego State. Other victories included 25-17 over Oklahoma State, 24-3 against Auburn, and 23-21 over Virginia Tech.

FSU was ranked nineteenth in the nation and 8-2 going into their final game of the regular season with the Florida Gators on December 3 in Jacksonville. The Gators were 6-3-1 and coming off a 17-point win against Miami. And the Gators had won the previous nine meetings between the two teams. By that year Florida dominated the rivalry 16-2-1.

"Some of the alumni here think if you win all your other games and lose to Florida, you're not successful," Bobby Bowden said.

The Seminoles started two quarterbacks equally that year, Jimmy Jordan and Wally Woodham. During FSU's first drive against the Gators, Woodham threw a touchdown pass to Kurt Unglaub. Later in the first half, Jimmy Jordan connected with Roger Overby for six. FSU led 17-9 at halftime.

In the second half, Jordan threw two more touchdown passes to Overby, securing the 37-9 victory.

"That was one of the biggest games I had ever played in," Bobby said. "It had been awhile since we had beaten them. It felt good. But Coach Bowden would beat them a lot more after that game my senior year."

The Seminoles finished 10-2 overall, including beating Texas Tech University 40-17 in the Tangerine Bowl on December 23 in Orlando. With that win, FSU became the first major college football team in Florida to win ten games in a season. FSU took an early lead in the game on a 23-yard Dave Cappelen field goal.

The crowd of 44,502 saw FSU easily handle Texas Tech as the Seminoles' scores included a 93-yard kickoff return by Larry Key and four touchdown passes. FSU quarterback Jimmy Jordan became game MVP as he completed eighteen of 25 passes for 311 yards and two touchdowns.

"That was Coach Bowden's first bowl win at FSU," Bobby said. "Looking back, it was such a big win for us at the time and for the future of the program."

Following the bowl victory, FSU was ranked fourteenth in the nation by the Associated Press. Bobby finished his career with ten interceptions, surpassing the school's old record of eight, and selected Honorable All-American.

Bobby Bowden, one of the greatest collegiate coaches in history, won more than three hundred games at FSU, including two national championships, 1993 and 1999, before he retired in 2009. His tenure lasted thirty-four years.

Bobby Jackson became one of Bobby Bowden's first players from FSU to sign a professional contract. There'd be many more.

"Bobby became our leader on defense," Bowden said. "The first year under me, my first year there, he struggled a little bit. But his second year he became a pro."

*

Jimmie Callaway worked as equipment manager for most of Bobby Bowden's tenure at FSU, including when Bobby played under him. Callaway's friends called him "J.C." and Bowden called him "the toughest, orneriest sergeant in managerial history."

Callaway oversaw the equipment as if a lost chin strip could lead to imprisonment. A Tallahassee native, he fell in love with the Seminoles when he was a boy, and spent fifty years connected in various ways with the FSU football program.

At age twelve in 1947, he became the ball boy at the first FSU game in Tallahassee. He still has one of the balls used that day. Callaway has seen most of the home games at Doak S. Campbell Stadium in Tallahassee, named after the university's president when it opened by the early 1950s.

Callaway continued to follow the team closely after he retired as equipment manager in the late 1990s. The best player he ever saw at FSU was Deion Sanders, and he ranked Bobby Jackson in the top "four or five players" in the school's history.

Deion played cornerback from 1985 to 1988, had fourteen interceptions and became a two-time NCAA All-American. Known as Primetime, he is considered by many as one of the greatest two-sport athletes ever, playing both in the NFL and in Major League Baseball. He once hit over .300 for the Atlanta Braves, and in 1992 led the National League in triples. In 2011, he was inducted into the Pro Football Hall of Fame. Both Sanders and Jackson are remembered fondly by Callaway, not only for their athleticism, but how they carried themselves, the respect they gave to others.

"An equipment manager wants to know does a player complain," Callaway said. "For Bobby Jackson, no. He was always polite, always said thank you. He was just a great guy and never gave anybody any problem."

Some years ago, Callaway built a six hundred-square foot facility at his home in Tallahassee and created his own FSU museum. In it he has hundreds of pieces of memorabilia, including helmets, jerseys, and a football from the 1947 game in which he was a ball boy. Seminole pride since the 1940s.

*

Before Bobby completed his career at FSU, Coach Dan Henning had left the school and joined the coaching staff of the New York Jets. Henning said he wanted the organization to select Bobby in the upcoming 1978 NFL draft. Scouts from a few other teams, including the Dallas Cowboys and the Miami Dolphins, had watched Bobby work out in Tallahassee. But these teams had not expressed a lot of interest in him.

Henning had talked to the Jets, and some in the organization were concerned that Bobby was too small to play in the NFL. Henning told the Jets not to worry about Bobby's size and that he could start as a rookie for the team. Team officials were hesitant. Bobby remained confident.

Draft day came, and Bobby watched the event on television with his roommate, Michael Kincaid. After the fifth round he left the dorm becoming frustrated he had yet to be selected. Bobby had a meal and returned to his dorm. When he did, Michael handed him a piece of paper with a telephone number on it. The number belonged to Henning.

Bobby called Henning and learned he had been selected the first pick of the sixth round, 141 overall, by the Jets.

"Henning told me later he had told the Jets to draft me in the third round," Bobby said. "They were concerned about my size. I had missed only one out of forty-five games at FSU because of an injury. I knew I could play at the next level. At the time I was just upset I wasn't drafted higher."

He knew the reasons why. "In the back of my mind I could hear those voices" saying he was too small to play in the NFL, Bobby said. "That put a chip on my shoulders and took me back to one of Coach Archer's favorite sayings at Albany High: It's not the size of the dog in the fight, it's the size of the fight in the dog."

Bobby signed for an annual salary of thirty thousand dollars and an eleven thousand dollar bonus. He left FSU a few credits short of a degree in criminology but confident in his ability and desire to excel in the NFL.

CHAPTER 7

After the draft and in preparation for the Jets' mini-camp for rookies, Bobby did what he had done both in high school and at FSU. He worked. And he worked some more. He ran, lifted weights, and maintained the kind of diet conducive to athletic achievement.

When he arrived at the camp at Hofstra University on Long Island, team trainers found he had less than two percent body fat. No other player at camp had less body fat than he did. Plus, he had a hundred percent desire to prove himself and earn a starting position.

At five-foot nine and about 175 pounds, throughout his career with the Jets his height became purposely, and mistakenly, listed at five-ten or even five-eleven.

"When that happened, it meant they had stretched me," Bobby said.

The three-day camp in May went well for Bobby. He showed excellent defensive coverage and coaches clocked him at 4.5 seconds in the forty-yard dash, the fastest at camp. He did experience some cramping in his legs on the final day and did not participate.

"When I left there, I was ready for the camp with the veterans," he said. "I felt like I had a good mini-camp and wanted to show the coaches what I could do against the veterans."

After camp, Bobby returned to his home in Albany to train for another month. He became determined to improve his time in the forty. And determined to fight for a starting position.

He came back for the opening of regular pre-season camp in mid-July and was timed at 4.4 in the forty-yard dash, tying wide receiver Wesley Walker and running back Charlie White for the team's best. His defensive coverage remained excellent, his physical play relentless, and he once got into a shoving match with veteran and All-Pro Rich Caster, who had played both tight end and wide receiver.

At six-foot five and 230 pounds, Caster had been with the Jets since they drafted him in 1970 after his career at Jackson State University. Like Bobby, he was from the South, having been born in Mobile, Alabama. Caster, in 1978, eventually left the Jets and joined the Houston Oilers. He finished his NFL career with the Washington Redskins.

The shoving incident at camp occurred during drills, when Caster pulled up on a passing route and blocked Jackson. "It wasn't a fight," Bobby said. "I was trying to prove something. I was trying to make the team. He was a veteran and already had a spot on the team. I was just showing those guys that I wasn't going to back down from anyone."

At camp, no matter what the size of his teammates he was battling, he would not be intimidated. After the first week, Bobby had earned the close attention of the coaching staff. Then the team released cornerback Billy Hardee, who had started the previous season. Bobby had earned a starting position and would keep it for the entire season. And the next seven.

During camp in 1978, one New York newspaper included this in a story about the promise of Bobby Jackson:

> Defensive backfield coach John Mazur said speed is the No. 1 requirement but that Jackson also has "quickness and ability" to go with it, and that makes him valuable... "He's a quick, young guy, and he's aggressive," free safety Burgess Owens said. "He's a gusty little guy. Vets may get teed off at him for a minute or so, but you've got to respect the way he plays."
>
> Jackson said he has always tried harder because of his size. "They wouldn't let me play football in junior high (in Albany, Ga.) because they said I was too small," he said. "I played sandlot, made the high school team and was all-state

as a wide receiver and cornerback. I wasn't any taller than I was in junior high, either."

He still has a baby face and could easily be mistaken for a 16-year-old if not for his mustache and goatee. "The goatee just came, and I left it," he said, "but I grew the mustache a couple of years ago to look older. Hey, when I'm 40 I'll still look young. It's not so bad having a baby face."

Two years before the Jets drafted Bobby, they had selected Shafer Suggs from Ball State University in Muncie, Indiana, who played strong safety. Bobby and Shafer were teammates for three years.

"Bobby came into camp and made an immediate impact," Shafer said. "And he had an attitude and demeanor that fit right in. We used to call him, 'Bobby Bad Ass,' and he didn't shy away from that name."

Shafer had grown up in a two-parent middle-class family in Elkhart, Indiana, where he had excelled in football and basketball in high school. His parents had him involved in Soap Box Derby and Boy Scouts, and a few blacks - there were not many in Elkhart - sometimes said Shafer was "trying to act white," he said. Bobby, of course, had had a much different childhood. The two became friends.

Shafer later played with the Cincinnati Bengals, the Montreal Alouettes of the Canadian Football League, and the New Jersey Generals with the old United States Football League. After his football career ended in 1983, he worked for thirty years as a senior-level executive for a few companies, including Motorola and Cintas, which sells work uniforms. As of 2014, Shafer was serving on the executive board of the Chicago Chapter of the Former NFL Players Association.

"Bobby and I hit it off early on, and I sort of mentored him," he said. "Even went with him once to help him buy a car."

Bobby said, "Living in New York was a big change for me. I became close to Shafer and some of my other teammates then, and we're still close today. They helped me adjust to big-city life."

Shafer had watched closely several rookies as they came into the league. Some made it and some didn't. Bobby didn't fit what Shafer had seen from other NFL rookies.

"He wasn't the typical rookie," Shafer said. "He carried himself with a great level of arrogance that went along with playing his position."

During one scrimmage, running back Clark Gaines took a handoff and burst through the line of scrimmage as Bobby came up to hit him hard and make the tackle. Clark tried to run over and punish Bobby. Clark was from Elberton, Georgia, had played at Wake Forest, and had rushed for more than 700 yards during his rookie season in 1976 with the Jets.

"Bobby hit so hard all the time," Shafer said, "but on that hit against Clark he learned that others can hit, too. He came back to our huddle after that and said, 'That bitch was tough!' "

Once, during a game against the Chicago Bears, Bobby took a powerful forearm from running back Walter Payton, Shafer said. But he made the tackle.

"Bobby took some tough licks because guys knew that he was out to get them," Shafer said. "For his size, he was probably one of the hardest hitting cornerbacks in the league back then. If he had played on a winning team, no doubt he would've been All Pro. He would've gotten more recognition, which was what he deserved."

At his first full Jets training camp at Hofstra University, Bobby saw the exceptional speed of wide receiver Wesley Walker. The Jets drafted Walker in the second round out of the University of California at Berkeley in 1977, and he would play his entire career with the team, retiring in 1989. At six-foot three and 175 pounds, Walker was one of the premier wide receivers in the NFL. For his career he had 438 receptions for around

8,306 yards, and seventy-one touchdowns.

During Bobby's rookie year in 1978, Wesley had forty-eight receptions and eight touchdowns. He led the NFL that season with 1,169 reception yards.

While Bobby sized up Wesley at some of the early practices in '78, Wesley was doing the same to Bobby. Wesley soon realized, as did Shafer and other teammates, Bobby was going to be an immediate impact player for the Jets. And the defensive backfield would improve because of him.

Wesley's speed was equal to Bobby's, but his eyesight was not. While he was catching all those passes, and scoring all those touchdowns, doctors had determined that Walker was legally blind in his left eye. Bobby came to admire Walker for overcoming his adversity, and for the precise way he ran passing routes and caught balls. Always elusive after the ball was snapped and he had begun his route.

They became friends off the field. On the field, their relationship was more than mutual admiration. Having one of the league's best receivers on his team helped make Bobby a better defender. And with the arrival of Bobby Jackson, Wesley Walker would now be challenged in practice in a way that he had not been, elevating his game, making him a better receiver.

"During camp in my mind if I could cover Wesley Walker," Bobby said, "I could play in the NFL. He made me a better ball player. I made it a point to cover him at practice, and he obviously had great speed. When I covered him, my confidence went up."

Wesley was considered one of the best deep threats in the league, the kind of receiver who'd "eat your cushion up so fast" coming off the line of scrimmage. The "cushion" Bobby referred to is how much space, or yardage, off the line of scrimmage a cornerback gives a receiver before the play begins. The farther back a defender is from a receiver generally indicates greater respect that defender has for the receiver's speed, quickness, and ability to execute a route.

Bobby found, from the collegiate to professional level, wide receivers were more precise with their patterns, leaving no room for error from a defensive perspective.

Bobby gave an interview to one reporter during his first full pre-season camp at Hofstra, as he was leaving the dormitory on the way to the practice field.

"Let's go play in the traffic," he said. "Out on the corner where I am, they call it the expressway. Things happen there in a hurry. You've got to have good wheels. You've got to watch out for the linemen as big as buses. You've got to anticipate what the other guy is going to do before he does it."

The same story quoted Coach Michaels as listing Bobby one of the most impressive newcomers at camp, along with tackle Chris Ward, tight end Mickey Shuler, middle linebacker Mark Merrill, and fullback Jim Early. "Jackson is quick and he's learning," Michaels said. "He has shown good hands most of the time."

If being a cornerback in the NFL was like working on the expressway, part of Bobby's work crew included Wesley Walker.

"There's no question that Bobby was one of the best corners in the league." Wesley said later. "People used to say to me, who was the best defensive back I went against? It was Bobby. He prepared me to be my best, and there's no question he made me a better player."

In 2014 Wesley was living on Long Island, New York, where he stayed after his football career ended and taught physical education for elementary students in the public schools for about twenty-five years. He said he suffers daily "constant, wrenching pain" from the thirteen years he played in the NFL.

Since retirement he has been operated on five times for in-

juries related to football, including spinal and shoulder surgeries. At one point, because of the pain, he went through a long
period of alcohol abuse, but was able to overcome it.

Before Wesley's physical problems began and when he was
one of the best receivers in the NFL, Bobby practiced against
him, giving no cushion at the line of scrimmage. This was a
period when the league allowed more contact between receivers
and defenders, as opposed to today. Helmet-to-helmet tackles
were also within the rules. With Bobby, "You had to win the
line of scrimmage to beat him," Wesley said. "That was always
hard to do."

Bobby was one of the few corners in the league for which
Wesley said he had to be wholly focused coming off the line of
scrimmage to compete against him.

"Bobby was as good as Lester Hayes," Wesley said. "I could
do things against Lester I couldn't do against Bobby."

Lester played in the Pro Bowl five times and was part of the
Oakland Raiders' Super Bowl victories in 1980 and '83. Bobby
finished his career without being selected to the Pro Bowl or
making it to the Super Bowl.

"I'm not taking anything away from Lester," Wesley said.
"He was on a winning team. Bobby was just as good if not better. Sometimes you don't get the recognition you deserve unless
you're on a winning team, and sometimes it's about perception
and popularity."

The toughness that marked Bobby's days at Albany High
and FSU, revealed itself to Wesley and the rest of the Jets. "He
was just tough physically and when we practiced, it was just a
fight, day in and day out," Wesley said. "In the end, we helped
each other become better."

Wesley and his teammates, by the third pre-season game of
1978, saw a play that epitomized Bobby's toughness as the Jets
were playing the San Diego Chargers in California. *The Hit,*
and there would be others like it, came to symbolize Bobby's
fearlessness on the field.

San Diego's fullback, William "Bo" Matthews from Huntsville, Alabama, played at the University of Colorado before the Chargers drafted him in the first round in 1974. He was six four and about 230 pounds.

During the game, he caught a flair pass coming out of the backfield on the opposite side of the field from Bobby. The young cornerback, only twenty-one at the time and the youngest player on the team, gave pursuit to make the tackle along the sidelines. The play unfolded in front of the New York bench. Matthews may have thought he could easily run over Bobby, out-weighing him by sixty pounds. He kept coming and so did Bobby.

"We hit head on," Bobby said. "I had probably run full speed forty yards. They had to wake him up in front of our bench and stop the game to revive him. I was seeing three of him and was dizzy for a few minutes. But that was the moment my teammates begin to respect me."

Bobby had done this kind of hitting since high school in Albany, when he knocked out one of his teammates during practice and did the same to an outstanding wide receiver, Billy Dixon, who played for nearby Crisp County High School. Twice in the early '80s in the NFL, he put crushing hits on fullbacks who went down, stayed down, and eventually had to be helped up by their teammates.

One of those came against his old rival William Andrews, who played for Thomasville High School and Auburn University, and later with the Atlanta Falcons. The other came against Booker Moore, who played for the Buffalo Bills in the early 1980s.

Moore, a 225-pound fullback from Flint, Michigan, played at Penn State University before joining the Bills. Like Matthews at San Diego, Moore caught a flair pass coming out of the backfield and Bobby came hard to make the tackle.

"When I hit him, I knocked him backwards and he fell down," Bobby said. "I hit the ground hard but got up and started celebrating. But then I blacked out. I didn't play the second half. Everything was in slow motion and blurry."

After Moore's NFL career, he returned to Flint and spent several years working as a deputy in the Genesee County Sheriff's Department. He died of a heart attack in 2009 on a Sunday, while watching football on television.

Bobby hit the way he did to tell opposing receivers not to run a route on his side of the field. He wanted them to think more about him and the violent way he could hit, and less about catching the ball, he said. Johnny "Mule" Coleman had taught him to play that way during sandlot ball in the public housing neighborhoods in Albany, Georgia. Bobby never forgot the lesson.

He played that way during high school and college. Football is supposed to be played that was, he said. Always undersized and sometimes overlooked because of his size, every opportunity to hit an opponent became an opportunity to show others he belonged in the NFL. To show others the full range of his desire and physical powers.

Bruce Harper, a running back with the Jets from 1977-84, played at Kutztown State in New Jersey. Bruce and Bobby were similar in size. But he said his thoughts were more about "survival" than hitting opponents the way Bobby did.

"The first thing I remember about Bobby on the football field was *nasty, nasty*," Bruce said. "I literally seen him knock out – on his own – two guys much bigger than him."

Bruce said he saw Bobby develop as a player and become a leader and defensive captain in 1981. In the locker room, Bobby and other defenders shared a space they called "The Ghetto," Bruce said. "They were just crazy defensive guys who had fun together. They were tight. I referred to Bobby as our shut-down corner."

That Jets' defensive unit would eventually include Jerry Holmes, who played cornerback and free safety from 1980-83. Jerry also played for West Virginia University. He finished his NFL career with the Green Bay Packers in 1991. Since then he has coached at both the professional and collegiate levels, and by 2014 became defensive coordinator for Virginia State University.

"The one thing about Bobby I remember was that he was a true leader," Jerry said. "How he worked at practice set an example for the rest of us. He always had intensity. Always competing at practice, even when we ran sprints. He was my mentor."

*

On July 25, 1978, the *New York Times* published a story with this headline, 'New Jets Cornerback Expected to Solve a Longtime Problem.' The story said Bobby would certainly make the team because he was faster than all the receivers, and had a thirty-two-inch vertical jump, higher than any of his teammates. The Jets the year before, the story reported, finished last in pass defense of the twenty-eight NFL teams. They needed help.

The story accurately listed Bobby at five-foot nine and 175 pounds. The paper also quoted Bobby concerning his height, or lack of it as some might argue. "The only time I can see height as a factor is in a goal-line situation, when a quarterback might lob the pass. But I figure if the receiver can get to it, I can get to it." The article continued:

> The Jets have traditionally been talent-poor in the secondary. No one can remember the last time they had a secondary unit intact for two consecutive years. Jackson appears to be insuring himself for the job at left corner. One way, he said, is "to get the receiver thinking about you and not the ball; I upset them anyway I can." That intimidation

does not extend to Rich Caster and Wesley Walker. "They don't want you to hurt the veterans."

Along with being one of the smallest Jets at his first pre-season camp in 1978, Bobby was the youngest at 21. But Head Coach Walt Michaels had seen enough at camp not to be concerned about either his size or his age. After the Jets drafted him, Michaels got several telephone calls from college coaches who played against Bobby. They told Michaels he had picked an excellent football player who would likely have an immediate impact on his team.

Michaels became convinced at pre-season camp that those coaches were correct, and Bobby only needed experience at the professional level to become an outstanding player.

Michaels told a newspaper reporter this: "We feel Bobby Jackson is going to be around for a long time." The experiences on the field came quickly. And Michaels' prediction held true as Bobby became an eight-year starter for the Jets and helped re-vitalize their defense.

Michaels, born in 1929 in Swoyersville, Pennsylvania, played football at Washington & Lee University. The Cleveland Browns drafted him in 1951. Before the season started, Cleveland traded him to the Green Bay Packers where he played one season, primarily on specialty teams. Then he returned to the Browns for the '52 season and played linebacker there until he retired from football after the '61 season. That year the league expanded to fourteen from twelve regular season games.

At six feet and 230 pounds, Michaels hit hard on the field and had a reputation as a great tackler. Bobby Jackson played the same way. Michaels made the Pro Bowl five consecutive years beginning in 1955. Playing under head coach Paul Brown, the Cleveland Browns were in five championship games and won two. After retiring as a player, Michaels became the secondary coach for the Oakland Raiders of the American Football League.

He was the Jets' defensive coordinator in 1969 during one of the biggest upsets in football history, as the Jets of the AFL, led by quarterback Joe Namath, defeated the NFL's Baltimore Colts 16-7. Michaels became the Jets' head coach in '77.

*

Jets' wide receiver coach Den Henning, who had recruited Bobby to play that position at FSU, told a New York reporter he remembered Bobby coming to FSU when he was seventeen, looking too young to play college football. Bobby surprised a lot of people in Tallahassee by his intensity on the football field, Henning said. His accomplishments in the NFL would not surprise Henning.

"He was something to watch," Henning said of Bobby's arrival at FSU. "He covered our varsity receivers man-to-man. He was the best cornerback on the field."

Henning, born in 1942 in the Bronx, played quarterback at the College of William & Mary in Virginia. By the mid-1960s he played for the San Diego Chargers. He began coaching in the late '60s, and spent many years doing so at both the professional and collegiate levels.

Henning, head coach of the Atlanta Falcons from 1983 to '86, signed Bobby to his last professional contract in 1986. While the head coach of Boston College in the mid-1990s, Henning discovered and made public a major sports betting scandal among his players, resulting in the suspension of about a dozen of them.

*

The Jets first regular season game in 1978 came on September 3 at Shea Stadium where they defeated the Miami Dolphins 33-20. Hometown fans saw Bobby knock down two passes, one in his own end zone, and almost intercepted an overthrown pass by quarterback Don Strock. Bobby made a hard tackle, "putting his shoulder" to running back Delvin

Williams, reported the *Albany Herald*, his hometown newspaper.

The paper said, "the baby-faced Jackson, who sports a moustache and goatee to hide his youthful look, is all muscle, with Popeye-like arms that house 17-inch biceps, and can bench press 325 pounds."

Fans had reason to be excited after the opener because the Jets had gone 3-11 the year before and given up twenty-three touchdown passes, finishing last in the league in pass defense.

Along with Bobby, the defensive backfield in 1978 included, Reggie Grant, University of Oregon; Tim Moreso, University of Syracuse; Burgess Owens, University of Miami; Larry Riley, Salem State University in Massachusetts; Ken Shroy, University of Maryland; Shafer Suggs, Ball State University in Indiana; and Ed Taylor, University of Memphis.

In preparation for the sixth game of the season, defensive secondary coach John Mazur conducted a meeting with his players and used a blackboard to help convey his message "to be more aggressive and stop worrying about the bomb."

The Jets, 2-3 going into the game, defeated the Buffalo Bills 45-14 at Shea Stadium in front of 44,545 fans with "a daring, gambling restructuring of the defensive philosophy," one newspaper reported.

Bobby and fellow cornerback Ed Taylor were instructed to play bump-and-run. Win or lose, man against man. Bobby limited wide receiver Bob Chandler to one reception, a 15-yard touchdown pass from Bill Munson with twenty-eight seconds left in the game. Taylor held Bills' wide receiver Frank Lewis to one catch as well. Free safety and defensive captain Burgess Owens ran an interception back for a 40-yard Jets touchdown.

Bobby had his first NFL interception and twenty more would follow before he retired. The Jets had a new defensive philosophy.

John Mazur, born in 1930 in Plymouth, Pennsylvania, played quarterback for Notre Dame when the school became national champions in 1949. After college, Mazur played briefly with the British Columbia Lions of the Canadian Football League. He became head coach of the New England Patriots in the early 1970s. Mazur died in 2013 of complications related to Parkinson's disease.

Burgess Owens grew up in Tallahassee and played at the University of Miami before the Jets drafted him in 1973. He played for the Jets until '79 and joined the Oakland Raiders in the early '80s. Throughout his NFL career, he said one of the toughest interceptions he made was against his teammate, Bobby Jackson.

"We were playing the Raiders and Kenny Stabler threw a ball in the end zone," Burgess said. "I don't know what happened to the receiver. I went up for the ball and had to fight Bobby to get it. It should've been all mine. But that's the way he was. He was just that competitive."

With Bobby, the Jets' defensive backfield became more aggressive, Burgess said. "There are different styles of corners. Bobby would not hesitate to come up and make a big hit. Some corners don't like to do that. Bobby wasn't one of those."

Bobby and Burgess were both black men who grew up in the Deep South and came out of a period of intense racial discrimination. They became friends and later, when their careers ended, business partners for a few years. But they spoke little about the South and its ugly racial history, Burgess said.

"I think both of us appreciated what we had accomplished" and didn't dwell on the racism they and the South had experienced. "I like to point to guys like Bobby, who grew up in a small town with not a lot of opportunities," Burgess said. "He worked hard and was able to stand out. To me it's the American Dream. He never took anything for granted. When you're the underdog, you have no problem doing the extra work and proving people wrong."

The Jets finished the year 8-8, third place in the AFC behind Miami and the New England Patriots. They beat both Miami and the Baltimore Colts twice that year. Bobby had five interceptions his rookie year, tied for the team lead with Burgess. Wide receiver Wesley Walker, who challenged Bobby regularly at practice, became the team's only Pro Bowl selection. Michaels was selected AFC Coach of the Year for keeping the youngest team in the NFL in playoff contention for fifteen weeks.

Bobby started every game and made the AFC All-Rookie Team as a starter. "I felt like I had made an impact," he said. "And our team was young and had improved from the year before. Our pass defense was better."

Team passing defense, last in the league in 1977 out of 28 teams, improved to 23rd in '78. With so many good young players, the team's future looked good.

CHAPTER 8

For about twelve years Bobby had no contact with his mother, Donna Mae Meeks. She had chosen not to reach out to her son, to let him live his life without her, as she lived hers, focusing on her four other children, she said. She eventually regretted her decision.

Bobby had been hurt by her absence and often thought about her. That changed unexpectedly in the Mineola Courthouse in Mineola, New York, not long after he was drafted by the Jets.

Donna Mae, whose own mother had died of natural causes in the 1980s, came to the courthouse that day in support of Tyrone Smith, a man from Cocoa Beach, Florida, she had been living with for a few years. At Tyrone's urging, the couple had moved to New York. But Tyrone had "gotten with the wrong crowd" and had been arrested for armed robbery, she said. Tyrone eventually served about seven years in prison.

The same day Donna Mae arrived at the courthouse, Bobby had done so in support of a friend who had legal problems of his own.

While sitting and waiting at the courthouse, Bobby saw a woman who reminded him of his mother. He told his friend to approach the woman and ask her if she was from Albany, Georgia, and did she have a son named Bobby Jackson. The friend did what Bobby asked.

"I looked back over at Bobby and he was smiling," Donna Mae said. "I'd recognize that smile anywhere."

In that courthouse that day their relationship, of talking and spending time together, began anew and endures today.

"I apologized to him for staying away for so long, and he accepted," Donna Mae said.

Bobby accepted his mother's apology for the many years of absence and holds no resentment toward her, he said.

"She was just sixteen when she had me," he said. "I was young when I had my first child, and I know what it's like to be a young parent."

Donna Mae lived on Long Island and had a job providing care for the elderly. She often visited Tyrone Smith in prison, and she and Bobby began spending time together after their courthouse reunion. Bobby often visited her at her home, and sometimes spent the night.

"It was just good for me to have my mother back," Bobby said.

When Bobby got married in 1983 and began having children, his mother often took care of his children when Bobby and his wife were away from their home. "For the first time I was beginning to know my son," Donna Mae said. "And to know my grandchildren."

She attended some of the Jets' games, and her family photo albums today contain a handful of pictures she took at Shea Stadium. She had not attended any of his high school or college games. Until their reunion in the courthouse, Donna Mae did not know her son played professional football. When she learned he did, she told him how proud she was of all his accomplishments, Donna Mae said.

"I wasn't there for the most important things in his life, but he doesn't seem to hold that against me," she said.

*

The Jets opened the 1979 season with an overtime loss to the Cleveland Browns, and during the second week were beaten 3-56 by the New England Patriots. Then they beat the Detroit Lions 31-10 and lost to the Buffalo Bills 31-46.

Game five on September 30 was at Shea Stadium where 51,496 fans saw the Jets against the Miami Dolphins, who came into the game undefeated.

During the closing minutes of the third quarter a big play for the Jets electrified the crowd. The *Daily News* called it a "brazen interception by cornerback Bobby Jackson" that he returned fifty-eight yards for a touchdown.

The Jets won 33-27, when quarterback Richard Todd and Wesley Walker combined for a 71-yard touchdown pass with about two minutes remaining.

Bobby's touchdown interception came off quarterback Bob Griese, who attempted a short, sideline pass to wide receiver Jimmy Cefalo. The *Daily News* recapped it this way:

> The tendency here might have been for left corner Bobby Jackson to play it safe and go for the tackle. The second-year pro had been burned as much as anyone this year. Why risk another big gainer? But Jackson was going for broke. He saw Griese taking an extremely short drop, only three steps. That meant a short pattern.
>
> "I was looking for something quick," Jackson said. "A quick post or a quick out. I could see the quarterback all the way and I got a good jump on the ball. At first I just worried about making the tackle, but when I got to him [Cefalo], I saw I had a shot at the ball and I took the shot."
>
> Even though he knew he was supposed to have deep support from the safety, Jackson knew he was taking a risk in going for the interception. But he went ahead and stepped in front of Cefalo, snatched the ball and was home free. "They just went to my side too often," he said. "I knew sooner or later God would help me because I'm a better defensive back than I showed in New England."

Following the game, Bobby's teammate and defensive captain Burgess Owens said, "We just didn't allow the big play like we have been giving people. Bobby Jackson's touchdown swung the momentum for us. That was a big play." Bobby had three more interceptions that year.

On October 15, the Jets defeated the Vikings 14-7 at Shea Stadium, the first Monday Night Football telecast to originate from the New York City area. As they did in 1978, the Jets finished third in the AFC with an 8-8 record.

Fans had much to talk about as the season ended with three consecutive victories. They beat Baltimore 30-17, New England 27-26, and Miami 27-24.

The following year, 1980, the team fell to a disappointing 4-12, beating Atlanta once, Miami twice, and Houston once. Bobby had one interception for the season as the team lost several close games, including 14-17 Baltimore, 14-17 Cleveland, and 20-21 New Orleans. But he went through sixteen games without giving up a touchdown pass.

On September 21 at Shea Stadium, the Jets fell 37-27 to the San Francisco 49er's, as Jets' quarterback Richard Todd completed 42 of 60 passes for 447 yards and three touchdowns. Fullback Clark Gaines caught seventeen of those, setting a team record that still stands today.

"We were disappointed that year," Bobby said. "We knew we were a much better team than that. When we got to camp for the 1981 season, guys were motivated to work. We knew that year was going to be different. And it was."

In 1981 Bobby was selected to be the Jets' defensive captain, and the team finished 10-5-1, second in the AFC, and headed for the playoffs for the first time since 1969. On November 15, the Jets played New England in Foxboro, New Jersey, and were 4-4-1 going into the game.

About midway in the game, which the Jets won 17-6, running back Mosi Tatupu broke through the line scrimmage and Bobby charged toward him to make the tackle. Mosi played at the University of Southern California, and at six feet and around 230 pounds, spent fourteen seasons in the NFL. As Bobby lowered his body to make the tackle, Mosi tried to jump over him.

"When he jumped, his knee hit my right arm and it felt like it was broke," Bobby said.

Suffering intense pain, Bobby could not use his arm to tackle or defend receivers. He came out of the game after the play and met with team trainers. One of the trainers began taping a shin guard pad around Bobby's arm intending for him to return to the game.

"I told the guy how bad it hurt and finally they took me to the locker room and x-rayed it," Bobby said.

He did not return to the New England game. His broken arm required surgery to repair the damage. Screws were inserted into the bone and a second surgery a few weeks later removed them. Those were the only surgeries Bobby had in connection with football injuries. The team placed him on the injured reserve list, and he missed the remaining six regular season games.

"I couldn't stand not playing and up to that point in my career, I had not missed many games," Bobby said.

On December 20, their final regular season game, the Jets clinched a playoff spot for the first time since 1969, after defeating Green Bay 28-3. During the game the Jets recorded nine defensive sacks and finished the season with 66.

Defensive ends Joe Klecko and Mark Gastineau of the New York Sack Exchange, as the defense was referred to during that period, each recorded about twenty sacks for the season, placing them among the league's leaders.

The following week the Jets were set to play the Buffalo Bills in the Wild Card playoff game.

Bobby practiced with the team during the week leading up to the playoff game. He had a hard cast on his arm covered by thick foam. His right arm looked like a club, he said. He covered receivers, went through drills, but did not participate in any contact.

He said he thought he was ready for the playoff game, and the coaches said the same. Bobby started against the Bills but about midway through the game he made a tackle, re-injured his arm, and then came out of the game.

"I could cover," he said. "But I couldn't hit. My arm had not healed. It was just too soon coming off the surgery. I had a lot of pain that day."

The Jets fought back from a 24-0 deficit but lost 27-31. Buffalo's Bill Simpson intercepted Richard Todd's pass on his two-yard line in the final ten seconds of the game.

It took a few weeks for Bobby's arm to fully heal after that season. The following year a players' strike shortened the season, as the Jets advanced to one game away from the Super Bowl.

CHAPTER 9

In 1982, the Jets opened at home with a 28-45 loss against Miami. Then they won their second game of the year on September 19, beating New England 31-7. They did not play again until late November.

The NFL Players Association, led by their team representatives, struck on September 20 because of their disagreement over the distribution of revenue among league owners.

After the players agreed to strike, the owners declared a lockout from team fields, training rooms, weight rooms, and equipment rooms. The owners rejected the players' demand for 55 percent of gross revenues.

The league had just signed a five-year $2.1 billion television contract during a period in which NFL players' salaries were much less than those of the other major sports.

In contrast to the other sports, professional football players did not have unrestricted free agency that gave players more of an opportunity to sell their talents to the highest bidders. The NFL union did not argue for free agency, but sought a wage scale with incentive and performance bonuses.

A deal between the owners and the union in mid-November ended the strike after 57 days. The new five-year contract included severance packages to players upon retirement, modest salary increases, and immediate bonuses of $10,000-$60,000 depending on years of service in the league.

"I lost money each week during the strike but got it back once the new deal was reached," Bobby said. "I supported what we did as players. The strike back then did a lot to help future players."

During the strike, Jets' players had regular practices at Hofstra University. They used part of the university that was not an official Jets' training field, therefore abiding by the owners' lockout requirements. The daily practices included none of the coaches and were usually attended by all the players, Bobby said.

After finishing 10-5-1 in 1981, Booby said the team thought '82 would be the year they advanced to the Super Bowl. The practices during the strike indicated the team's determination to go further in the playoffs than they did in '81, Bobby said.

"We felt we had to be ready and that this was going to be one of our best opportunities to go all the way," he said. "We were without coaches, but guys worked hard at those practices."

As the strike shortened the '82 season and angered many fans, the Jets during this period established a new defensive scheme that improved their pass defense . It included the middle linebacker only playing about half of the defensive snaps and being replaced by a defensive back during passing situations. This change added more speed and agility to the defensive unit, Bobby said.

Of the twenty-eight teams in the league in 1982, the Jets finished tenth in overall defense and ninth in passing defense. Their offense rated third best in the league, fourth in rushing, and seventh in passing.

Because of the strike, the season included only nine regular games as opposed to sixteen. The Jets finished 6-3 and were bound for the playoffs. The league adopted a special sixteen-team playoff arrangement, and the Jets were the sixth-placed seed.

In '82 Freeman McNeil became the first Jets' player to lead the league in rushing with 786 yards on 151 carries for average of 5.2 yards. The Jets opened with a 28-45 loss to Miami at home, but the following week, they beat New England on the road 31-7.

Defensive end Joe Klecko hurt his leg during the New England game, and the injury caused him to miss the rest of the regular season and the post season.

"Initially this hurt the team, but we did have some depth on that team, some guys that stepped up when Klecko went down," Bobby said.

Stepping up for the injured Klecko were a handful of primarily young linemen the Jets used the remainder of the season and into the playoffs. They included Kenny Neil of Iowa State, who was drafted by the Jets in 1981, and Ben Rudolph of Long Beach State, drafted the same year as Neil. Barry Bennett had played at Concordia College in Minnesota and then for the New Orleans Saints for a few years before joining the 1982 Jets. Rookie Rusty Guilbeau of McNeese State also played some on the defensive line that year.

"We didn't really miss a beat" after Klecko's injury, Bobby said. "Abdul Salaam was really the unsung hero on that line. He was double-teamed a lot" allowing other guys to make tackles and sacks.

On December 18, 1982, the seventh game of the season, the Jets traveled to Miami. A victory there would've ensured a playoff spot, Bobby said. The Jets were leading 19-17 in the fourth quarter after a 40-yard field goal by Pat Leahy.

With 32 seconds left in the game, Bobby had deep man-to-man pass coverage and an opportunity to intercept. But he did not make the proper judgment as the pass hit him in the facemask, and he and the ball fell to the ground.

"Had I made that interception, we'd probably would've held on to win," Bobby said.

After the incompletion, Miami went ahead 20-19 and won the game on a 47-yard field goal by Uwe von Schamann with three seconds remaining.

The next week the Jets traveled to Minnesota, needing another win to secure a playoff spot. There Bobby had the best single-game performance of his career. Each day at practice the thought of not making that interception during the Miami game stayed in his mind as he prepared for the contest against the Vikings in Minneapolis at the Metrodome.

"It bothered me I didn't make that play against the Dolphins," Bobby said. "I was having a great week at practice and wanted to help the team. I just had one of those feelings all week long" that something good would happen.

During pre-game warm ups in Minnesota, Bobby approached Coach Michaels and told him he planned to score a touchdown during the game. Later Michaels had a pre-game interview and told the announcers what Bobby had told him about scoring a touchdown. The announcers shared the information to the television audience before the game began.

Bobby didn't score one, he scored two.

By the second quarter, the Jets had a 7-0 lead after McNeil's two-yard touchdown run and Leahy's extra point. During that period, the Vikings attempted a field goal but Mark Gastineau blocked it.

Free safety Darrol Ray, a second round Jets' pick in 1980 out of Oklahoma University, scooped up the blocked field goal. Ray eventually fumbled the ball and Bobby ended up with it.

"I got it on the first bounce and there was only one player with a chance at me and he missed," Bobby said. After racing 80 yards, Bobby crossed the end zone.

By the fourth quarter the Jets were up 35-14, putting the Vikings and quarterback Tommy Kramer in an all-passing situation. Out of the shotgun formation, Kramer threw a pass on Bobby's side of the field. He had short coverage, and because of the big lead, he played more aggressively than usual at the line of scrimmage.

Kramer bobbled the snap but recovered and threw the ball toward the sidelines. Bobby stepped in front of the receiver and intercepted the pass. Then he raced untouched for 77 yards and his second touchdown of the game.

"I could've fell down and got up and fell down again and still scored," Bobby said.

Bobby recorded another interception that game that did not result in a touchdown. The Jets won 42-14 and were bound for the playoffs.

HBO selected Bobby as the league's defensive player of the week. The Jets presented Bobby with five game balls after the Minnesota victory. He received two balls for the two interceptions, a defensive and offensive game ball, and one for the returned fumble for a touchdown.

Their final game that season, in which Bobby did not give up a touchdown pass, they lost 13-37 to the Kansas City Chiefs. Like 1981, they were bound for the playoffs.

During the first round, the Jets had a convincing 44-17 win over the Cincinnati Bengals in Cincinnati. They did it by overcoming an early 14-3 deficit, amassing 517 total yards on offense, and scoring 21 points in the fourth quarter.

Then they upset the Los Angeles Raiders 17-14 in LA and became known to some as "Road Warriors." The Raiders had finished the year 8-1 behind running back Marcus Allen, who gained 697 yards and scored eleven touchdowns.

Then the Jets headed to Miami to play for the AFC Championship, January 23, 1983, one game away from the Super Bowl. The last time and only time the Jets had advanced to the Super Bowl came in 1969 when they won Super Bowl III by defeating the Baltimore Colts. The Dolphins had last appeared in the Super Bowl in 1974 when they defeated the Vikings 24-7.

The early '70s had been exceptional years for the Dolphins. Following the 1971 regular season, the Dolphins lost Super Bowl VI to the Dallas Cowboys 24-3. But the next season they were undefeated and won Super Bowl VII 14-7 over the Washington Redskins. The Dolphins remain the only NFL team to win the Super Bowl with a perfect season. From 1970 through '74, Miami compiled a cumulative record of 65-15-1.

Throughout Bobby's career, the Jets and Dolphins generally played one another close. During the 1981 regular season, they tied 28-28 on October 4, but the Jets won 16-15 on November 22.

"We were confident going in to that playoff game in '82," Bobby said. "Overall we had played well against Miami the last few years. Our defense was clicking, and we had a high- powered offense."

Twice during the '82 season Miami had defeated the Jets, 45-28 and 20-19. Heavy rains came to Miami along with the big game. NFL rules required a tarpaulin be placed over a field during inclement weather before a game, Bobby said. But the Dolphins had left the field exposed to a long period of rain that, some observers said, produced a muddy swamp on the field.

"It became the infamous Mud Bowl," Bobby said.

To the Jets and their fans, the Dolphins had purposely left the field exposed to the rain in order to slow the Jets' offense. It worked. The Jets lost 0-14, as quarterback Richard Todd was 15-37 for 103 yards and five interceptions.

Jets' running back Freeman McNeil finished the game with only 46 yards rushing. Against Cincinnati on January 9, he had rushed for 202 yards, and the following week against the Raiders for 101 yards. In the AFC Championship Game the Dolphins had four turnovers, as 67,396 fans watched the Orange Bowl become the Mud Bowl.

Scoreless at halftime, but in the third quarter Miami quarterback David Woodley threw a short pass on third down along the sidelines caught by wide receiver Duriel Harris. Bobby defended Harris and a referee ruled the pass a completion.

Bobby said he clearly saw that Harris only had one foot in bounds, not the two needed under NFL rules for a completion.

"When the play was called, I just said '*Bull Shit!*'" Bobby said. "But I didn't say it to the referee. I had turned away from him, but he heard me."

The referee threw his penalty flag calling unsportsmanlike conduct on Bobby and costing the Jets fifteen additional yards from where the catch was made. This placed the ball on the seven-yard line. From there running back Woody Bennett took a handoff from Woodley and scored on the next play.

Had Harris been called out-of-bounds after his catch, it would've been fourth down and the Dolphins would've likely attempted a field goal, Bobby said.

Harris played at New Mexico State University, and the Dolphins drafted him in the third round in 1976. He spent nine seasons with Miami, most of his career. At Miami he recorded 4,534 receiving yards and eighteen touchdowns.

The second and only other score of that game came when Jets' quarterback Richard Todd threw an interception in the fourth quarter. The Jets had drafted Todd out of the University of Alabama in the first round, the same year the Dolphins selected Harris. Todd, a prolific passer, spent eight seasons with the Jets, totaling 20,610 yards and 124 touchdowns. He recorded a completion of 54.3 percent.

Todd rolled right and attempted a flair pass in his own backfield during the playoff game with Miami. Linebacker A. J. Duhe, from Louisiana State University, read the play correctly and rushed into the Jets' backfield. The ball hit Duhe's hands. He bobbled it, then regained control of it and ran untouched for 35 yards and the final score. Duhe had three interceptions that day.

After he scored, one of the television announcers said, "It is hard to believe that A. J. Duhe in six years in the NFL has only two interceptions. He has three today and that one for a touchdown."

Michaels said this about his team after the loss: "We were prepared, we just didn't execute properly. There are some days when you shouldn't get up in the morning. Today was one of those days."

He later complained, as did others, that the Dolphins had purposely left the field exposed during the hard rain in order to slow the Jets' offense. A point still being debated today.

Bobby and his teammates still feel the pain today of that '82 loss at the Orange Bowl. "It was a big disappointment not going on to the Super Bowl," he said. "We had gotten so close. We had all worked hard even during the strike. And I was disappointed I didn't make the Pro Bowl that year. Not even alternate. I'm like, *'How in the hell didn't I make All-Pro?'* I was hurt."

Bobby finished the season with five interceptions and tied with five others for second place in the league. Everson Walls of the Dallas Cowboys led the league with seven interceptions. Bobby and two other players, all with two touchdowns, tied for first for most non-offensive TDs.

Five of Bobby's teammates did make the Pro Bowl that year: center, Joe Fields; wide receiver, Wesley Walker; offensive tackle, Marvin Powell; running back, Freeman McNeil; and defensive end, Mark Gastineau, part of the New York Sack Exchange.

"I know sometimes I didn't get the same recognition as the Sack Exchange," Bobby said. "But it still hurt that I didn't make the Pro Bowl."

Super Bowl XVII took place January 30, 1983, at the Rose Bowl in Pasadena, California, where 103,667 fans watched the Washington Redskins defeat the Miami Dolphins 27-17. Redskins' running back John Riggins earned MVP honors rushing for 166 yards, including a forty-three-yard touchdown.

"It was tough not being in that game," Bobby said. "All we could do was look to next year."

In February 1983, the Jets fired Michaels, replacing him with offensive coordinator Joe Walton. Michaels and team president Jim Kensil argued incessantly and Kensil complained of Michael's temper tantrums, according to press reports.

During Michael's tenure as head coach, 1977-82, he compiled an overall 39-47-1 record. Bobby said he had enjoyed playing under Michaels, thought of him as a fair and decent man and a fine football coach.

"Coach Michaels was a great coach," Bobby said. "He treated me like a man and didn't try to over coach us."

Bobby said Michaels received unfair treatment and his firing, in the long run, hurt the team. After leaving the Jets, Michaels became head coach for the New Jersey Generals of the short-lived USFL. He never returned to the NFL.

Bobby described Walton as a "control freak" whose coaching style was volatile, like "Dr. Jekyll and Mr. Hyde," and that Walton hurt the closeness of the team. Walton began a process of cutting players who he believed to be loyal to Michaels and not him, Bobby said.

Defensive lineman Marty Lyons had played at the University of Alabama and became part of the New York Sack Exchange. Like several players, he said he wanted Michaels to stay after the '82 season.

"I truly believe that if Walt had stayed we would have won a Super Bowl because he had already gotten us so close," Lyons said. "He was an intimidating coach. I remember being very intimidated by him my rookie year. He didn't care about players' personalities in the locker room. He played everything straight."

Lyons, drafted by the Jets in '79, played his entire career with them through the '89 season. That Super Bowl victory that he, Bobby, and others from that era had longed for did not come. Still hasn't come.

All-Pro wide receiver Wesley Walker said he had a lot of respect for both Walt Michaels and Joe Walton and expressed disappointment when Michaels was fired. He said he felt Michaels respected the players and had good football knowledge. But his view of Walton began to change once he became head coach.

"Walton tried to control too many things," Wesley said.

As an assistant coach, Walton had motivated players but with his promotion he became a "de-motivator," Wesley said. And whether Walton released players who were not considered loyal to him remains questionable. As successful as the team had been in '82, players as a whole were not close. There were cliques among the players, sometimes along racial lines.

"Behind my back I know I was referred to as a nigger," Wesley said.

A native of San Bernardino, California, Wesley had married a white woman and at the time, he said, "I didn't think anything about race" until becoming a part of the Jets. "I felt like if we had been more together as a team, we would've been better. It's hard to say how big a factor race was" in terms of hurting team unity.

The Jets of the early '80s had different factions among players, not unlike other teams, but overall was a "pretty tight" group, Bobby said. On any team it's natural for guys to gravitate to their teammates they feel comfortable being with away from the field and away from the locker room. Sometimes race played a part with the Jets, and sometimes it didn't.

Bobby said he never had any white teammate use a racial epithet around him. But some guys did make negative comments about the fact Wesley had married a white woman. "I do remember that," Bobby said. "Obviously Wesley will see race relations on the team from a different perspective from me."

In the Jets' locker room all of the defensive backs were assigned lockers together and named their area the "Ghetto." Not because they were all black except Ken Schroy, a white player, but because they were some of the lowest paid players on the team.

Schroy had played at the University of Maryland, and the Philadelphia Eagles drafted him in '75. Often seen hanging out with the players from the Ghetto was defensive end Mark Gastineau, part of the well-known New York Sack Exchange.

"Gastineau didn't belong in any group," Bobby said. "We kind of took him in. He wasn't really accepted by the established white players."

Gastineau's big ego sometimes turned his teammates away from him when the games and practices had ended, Bobby said.

*

As an active player for the Jets and since his retirement from the NFL in '86, and especially because he was selected for the All-Time Jets Team, Bobby has made countless appearances on behalf of the Jets' organization. He continues to live on Long Island. He has remained faithful and grateful to the Jets for drafting him, although not as high in the draft as he had hoped for.

"I get asked to do a lot of events even today," Bobby said. "But I enjoy it. I get to be with my old teammates and follow the new guys coming up. It's a lot of fun to me. I always want to do what I can for the team."

One such event occurred in June 2015, when the team asked Bobby and four of his teammates from the '82 season to come to the Atlantic Health Jets Training Center. With Bobby came linebacker Greg Buttle, wide receiver Wesley Walker, running back Bruce Harper, and defensive end Mark Gastineau. The five former Jets were asked by current head coach Todd Bowles and general manager Mike Maccagnan to attend a morning practice session.

That afternoon the former Jets signed five hundred white and green mini-helmets the organization planned to give away to fans during the upcoming season. And they dined with the team as the '82 highlight video played on monitors. Each of the five played together on six consecutive teams, from 1979-84.

The five were interviewed by a reporter concerning the '82 season and the AFC Championship Game with Miami. Some of what was said reflected Wesley's view that the team then was not as close a unit as it should've been. That year Gastineau had ten sacks, including four in the three post-season games. He spoke of regret:

> You want to talk about that season? I wanted to for-get about that one. That was a tough one. I really haven't watched any of it. I was more of a single person then, play-ing for myself, you know, selfish? Now I'm selfless. So you know, a lot of those memories I just use for kids today to tell them not to do the same things I did – and even these kids out here [current Jets].

Gastineau became the most high profile of the New York Sack Exchange that included Joe Klecko, Marty Lyons, and Abdul Salaam. In '81 the foursome recorded fifty-four and a half sacks. Five straight seasons, 1981-85, he played in the Pro Bowl. At six-foot five and 275 pounds, his self-promotion dance ritual after a quarterback sack was one of the reasons the league began to prohibit such antics in '84.

Bobby told the reporter in 2015 the Jets were definitely a Super Bowl-ready team in '82:

> That's what we thought after beating the Raiders out there. We felt we had beaten the best team in the AFC, and we beat the number one offense in Cincinnati that first week. We blew them out. Unfortunately, none of us even saw the field at the Orange Bowl until it was time to play.

The tarp rule came into effect because of that, but it was too late for us. My thought process was that Miami played on the same field we did so no excuses, they won. We had too many turnovers that game. We got a lot of turnovers, but basically we couldn't get in the end zone.

Bobby said the Dolphins purposely violated the "tarp rule" by not covering the field with a tarp to protect the ground against the heavy rain. A sloppy field made it much tougher for the high-powered Jets' offense that included speedsters Wesley Walker and Freeman McNeil.

The Dolphins finished the regular season 7-2 and first in the AFC East Division. Miami was 27th in passing offense in '82, but third in rushing. They were second in team defense, first in passing defense, and 24th in rushing defense. In seven of their victories, four opponents were held to ten or fewer points.

Jets linebacker Greg Buttle, part of the '82 team and with Bobby in June of 2015 at the Jets training facility said:

It was a pretty stupid season because of the strike, but we came back, and it was like we almost couldn't do anything wrong unless we played Miami, because we lost to them three times. We had a really good football team, and I think overall the Dolphins in the championship played better than we did and obviously it was a pretty good game going into halftime, but it is what it is.

It was a great run, and part of it was Walt Michaels. His comments to the team before the game and after the game were interesting and they were needed. There was no rah-rah stuff. He said, 'This is your chance, a one-in-a-million chance for you guys. Let's do it.' Walt had been to championship games before. He knew what it was about, and he wanted all the players to experience it.

Besides the championship game against Miami in '82, Wesley Walker talked about the playoff game against the Raiders a week before they lost to the Dolphins. In the 17-14 upset win, Wesley caught seven passes for 169 yards, including a twenty-yard touchdown. And he caught a 45-yard pass from Todd that ended on the Raiders' one-yard-line. From there, running back Scott Dierking scored with 3:45 left, giving the Jets the victory. Here's what Wesley said:

> …I'm going against Lester Hayes I just remember catching a pass that I was hoping was a touchdown to kind of turn the game around and we ended up scoring. But Lance Mehl, the linebacker, had a great game with two interceptions and turned it around. We were just on a roll, and those are the kind of games you want to be in and you want to be a part of.

*

The Jets finished 7-9 in '83 under their new head coach, while Bobby had two interceptions for the year. In October of that year, the Jets announced they were moving from Shea Stadium because it was "rundown, neglected and the NFL's poorest facility for athletes and spectators alike."

The team planned to begin the '84 season in the Meadowlands. Their last home game at Shea was December 10, 1983, when the Pittsburgh Steelers beat them 34-7.

During the '84 season Bobby played in only three games because of injuries, including a ruptured hamstring. The season ended the same way '83 had, with a disappointing 7-9 record. In February '84, the Jets traded quarterback Richard Todd to New Orleans for a first-round draft pick.

That year both Pat Ryan and Ken O'Brien split time at quarterback. Mark Gastineau had twenty-two sacks leading the league for the second straight year. This earned him his fourth Pro Bowl appearance.

Bobby's last couple of years with the Jets were marked by injuries, including to his left knee. He took multiple cortisone shots each game in order to ease the pain so he could play, he said. Pain in his neck and hamstrings were constant concerns toward the end of his career.

His body had taken a great deal of punishment since playing high school ball in the early '70s. All the hard hitting at each level of play had taken a heavy toll. By the mid-1980s, his foot-speed had slowed a bit, but he still had the desire necessary to compete in the NFL.

His final year with the team was '85. He had four interceptions but missed the last two games because of a knee injury. The Jets finished 11-5 and advanced to the playoffs for the third time since he had joined the team.

In January that year, former Jets' quarterback Joe Namath became the first player in franchise history to be elected to the Pro Football Hall of Fame in Canton, Ohio. And on October 14, during a nationally broadcast Monday Night game, Namath's number 12 was retired as the Jets defeated Miami 23-7.

Against Tampa Bay at home on November 17, the Jets set a club record for most points scored in their 62-28 win over Tampa Bay. The offense accounted for 581 total yards. Ken O'Brien threw five touchdown passes, three of them to tight end Mickey Shuler.

On December 8 at Buffalo during a 27-7 win, O'Brien connected with Wesley Walker for a 96-yard touchdown pass, the longest in club history. The team clinched a Wild Card playoff spot on December 22 with a 37-10 win over Cleveland.

Bobby could not play in the first-round playoff loss to New England, 14-26. "Finally my knee just gave out on me," he said. "I think it was against Buffalo late in the season. I had to come out of the game. They put me on injured reserve, and I was in street clothes watching the playoff game against New England."

During the game, the Jets had four turnovers, including a fumbled kickoff resulting in a Patriot touchdown.

*

Eight years as a starter with twenty-one interceptions, a key player who helped revitalize the Jets' defense, and one of the best corners in the league, Bobby covered some of the finest wide receivers in the NFL. Often, he covered them well. Occasionally he got beat. The ones who gave him the most trouble were those who were about his size and had his speed and his quickness.

Harold Jackson of the New England Patriots always challenged Bobby. At five-foot ten and 170 pounds, and from Hattiesburg, Mississippi, he played at Jackson State University. Jackson played seventeen seasons in the NFL, and in 1979 had 45 receptions for 1,013 yards and seven touchdowns. Jackson accounted for 10,372 reception yards and 76 touchdowns for his career.

Another Patriot receiver who was tough to cover, Bobby said, was Stanley Morgan. Like Bobby, he was not big, but fast, athletic, and quick off the line of scrimmage. An Easley, South Carolina, native, Morgan played fourteen seasons in the NFL after his career at the University of Tennessee. One of his best years in the NFL came in 1983, when he had 58 receptions for 863 yards and two touchdowns.

"Those two guys, Jackson and Morgan, were always a challenge for me," Bobby said. "I didn't have a problem with the big guys like Carmichael. It was the guys built like me who were tougher to cover. The ones with great speed and quickness."

Harold Carmichael, at six-foot eight and 225 pounds, played wide receiver in the NFL for fourteen years. A Jacksonville, Florida, native who played at Southern University, Carmichael had an outstanding year in '81 with the Philadelphia Eagles, when he had 61 receptions for 1,028 yards and six touchdowns.

Because of Carmichael's height advantage, Bobby struggled a bit defending him near the end zone and in the end zone itself. Space or the lack of it can sometimes work against a defender who is considerably shorter than the receiver.

"In the Red Zone, guys like Carmichael were a lot harder to cover," Bobby said.

At least once during his career, Bobby was beaten on a deep passing route by Mark Duper of the Miami Dolphins. The two were similar in height. Duper, a Moreauville, Louisiana, native, did not play high school football. He walked-on at Northwestern State University in Louisiana, before the Dolphins drafted him in the second round in 1982.

Duper's best time in the forty-yard dash as a professional was 4.26 seconds. He played eleven NFL seasons, all with Miami, and had a career 8,869 yards in receptions and 59 touchdowns.

"Bobby was a great cover back and he knew how to put himself in a position to cover," Duper said.

Duper referred to Bobby as an excellent "pre-reader," indicating his ability to watch both the receiver and quarterback and discern the upcoming pass route and how to correctly play it.

"Bobby always seemed to be in the right spot," Duper said.

Bobby intently studied game film before playing Miami, or any other team, in an effort to learn the habits of the receivers he covered, he said.

"I always thought he watched a lot of game film because he was so well prepared," Duper said.

He said he beat Bobby once on a long touchdown pass during a game in the mid-1980s, when he knew Bobby was playing with a pulled hamstring.

Bobby didn't start the game because of the injury, but he later replaced a teammate who was injured during the game, he said. Duper and quarterback Dan Marino connected for the pass.

"I knew he was hurt and Dan looked at me at the line of scrimmage, and we checked off on the play," Duper said.

The ball at first appeared to be overthrown, but Duper out-ran Bobby for the catch and the score. Duper, who owns a seventeen-acre horse ranch in Marksville, Louisiana, and Bobby established a friendship which remains intact today.

"I'm going to tell you if I had to pick the top ten corners in the NFL when I played, Bobby would be one of them," Duper said.

Bobby should've been a Pro Bowler, but the Jets' defensive line got a lot more attention than he did, Duper said. "There were a lot of times those guys made tackles because of Bobby's tough man-to-man coverage."

Duper and Bobby, along with the Jets and the Dolphins, were evenly matched during the early 1980s. "Every time we played, it was a dog fight," Duper said. "They would gear up for us."

One of Duper's teammates at Miami, Mark Clayton, matched Bobby's size as well. Clayton, an Indianapolis native, played at the University of Louisville. And he played eleven professional seasons, ten for Miami. He accounted for 8,974 career yards and 84 touchdowns.

"Those two guys were good, but you got to remember one of the best receivers I played against was Wesley Walker at practice," Bobby said. "He should be in the Hall of Fame. He helped prepare me for everybody else."

*

Bobby arrived in New York as a rookie in 1978 and became involved in a number of charitable activities during his tenure with the Jets, including speaking to schoolchildren about the dangers of using drugs. In 1985-86, he was selected as the Jets' representative to the United Way, and during that same period he and his wife Celeste received public service awards from the organization.

The attractive couple had filmed a public service announcement for United Way, and Bobby participated in a job-interviewing project for the Urban League of Long Island. A newspaper story quoted Bobby that when he first arrived in New York, he had fallen into the city's party scene for a few years. But by the mid-1980s he was more content to be at home with his wife and children, and volunteering his time to help others.

The newspaper reported that Bobby's name is more likely to be found on the guest list of a charity organization than, like some professional athletes, on a police report after being charged with a crime.

Throughout much of his career, he visited local hospitals, gave tickets to the Jets' games to troubled youngsters, and gave his time and financial help to various organizations. He said he wanted to be a good role model for children. He gave to others as he had been guided by his father, grandmother, and coaches at Albany High School. His own struggles with drug addiction came later, after he retired from the NFL.

*

After the 1985 season, Coach Walton called Bobby into his office for a conversation. Bobby said he "was surprised" by what Walton wanted to talk about.

"I got in his office and the first thing he said was, 'How's your family?' " Bobby said. "Then he told me I wasn't a part of the Jets' plans for next year. I was upset about the way it was all handled. I had given a lot to the team since they drafted me. The whole thing lasted just a few minutes. I basically just walked out the door when he said that to me. I still wanted to play, and I was only 28 years old."

His career with the Jets ended in seconds. Embittered and hurt by how it happened, Bobby still wanted to play in the NFL.

Walton played football at the University of Pittsburgh and play tight end for eight years for the Washington Redskins and New York Giants. He led the Jets through the '89 season when they finished 4-12. He compiled a 53-57-1 overall record after replacing Michaels. In the early 1990s, he spent a few years as offensive coordinator for the Pittsburgh Steelers. For twenty years, retiring in 2013, he was head coach at Robert Morris University, and recorded a 115-92-1 overall record.

Bobby said he had been loyal to Michaels and believed the Jets released him because of that loyalty. Walton began ridding the team of those who had backed Michaels. Before the '86 season began, Bobby went to San Francisco and worked out for the 49ers, who were interested in signing him. He also worked out with the Atlanta Falcons during this period.

"My health was better by then, but I wasn't a hundred percent," Bobby said. "I ran 4.55 in the forty. I knew I was faster than that." The 49ers offered Bobby a contract.

Bobby then got a call from Atlanta Falcons' head coach Dan Henning. "I had been with Henning at FSU and the Jets," Bobby said. "I always appreciated the way he coached. I signed a two-year deal with Atlanta. I thought Georgia, since I grew up there, would be a good place to end my career."

Bobby accepted a back-up role with the Falcons behind Bobby Butler. The two had been teammates at FSU. Bobby Jackson said he "was excited to again be on the same team with his friend and former teammate."

Butler, five-foot eleven and around 185 pounds, became Atlanta's first round draft pick in 1981. He played with the team until '92 and record 27 career interceptions.

"I was looking forward to playing with Bobby again," Bobby Jackson said. "It just felt right for me going to Atlanta then."

Bobby Jackson did start a game or two during the '86 preseason for Atlanta. But the injuries began to mount. The Falcons placed him on the injured reserve list, and it became apparent, a few games into the regular season, he would not be able to overcome his injuries and contribute to the team.

Henning released Bobby from the team. They both saw the irony in Henning's decision. But Bobby said he "laughed a little" with Henning about how his career ended.

Bobby fully understood the business side of football. He said he departed as friends with Henning, who, in 1978 while coaching with the Jets, urged them to draft Bobby when they were concerned about his five-foot nine stature.

"Dan Henning was the guy who started my career," Bobby said. "And he ended it. I've always appreciated that and always will."

After leaving the Falcons, he came to the realization his career was over. His body was through. "I was just tired of being hurt," he said. "But a part of me knew I could still play. It was all over then."

In 1987 the NFL players union struck again, and the Indianapolis Colts contacted Bobby, asking him if he'd be willing to play as a replacement player.

"I told them no thanks and that I wasn't going to cross the picket lines," he said. "I knew what those guys were fighting for."

About fifteen percent of NFL players did cross the picket line during the '87 strike. The players struck in late September, but games, after one week of cancellation, continued for a few weeks with primarily replacement players. The strike lasted only 24 days before the players agreed to return to work without gaining free agency concessions and without a new collective bargaining agreement. Bobby would not play football again.

CHAPTER 10

During his days with the Jets, Bobby and some of his teammates smoked marijuana, drank alcohol, and occasionally snorted cocaine as they partied in New York nightspots after practices and games. There were always girls. Plenty of girls.

His teammates referred to him as "Bo Love" because of his attraction to girls, and theirs to him. Bobby played hard on the field and the same way off of it when it was time to party. And there were always parties.

"Everybody smoked a little weed that played," Bobby said. "And sometimes we did a little cocaine."

Nothing he couldn't handle, he thought back then, he said. He kept himself in supreme physical shape during his NFL career. He controlled the drinking and the drug usage then. But after he retired, all of that would change. For a few years, these things would not only control him, but endanger his life and cause those who loved him to suffer.

During Bobby's rookie season in 1978, he met Celeste Serrano through teammate and defensive end Lawrence Pillers, a Mississippi native who played at Alcorn State University. Celeste, 21 at the time, knew some of the players through her work in connection with promotional parties she was involved in for the team.

They met at a fundraiser for the Miss Black America Pageant, founded in 1968 by J. Morris Anderson, in part to reverse the negative propaganda about black women during that period. Celeste worked at the organization when she met Bobby.

Celeste's beauty captured Bobby, while she found him both handsome and witty. Born in Brooklyn in 1957, Celeste had one sister and two brothers. Her father, Antonio Serrano, was born in Puerto Rico and owned a carpentry business. Her mother, Alberta Shelton Serrano, originally from Virginia and along with rearing her children, earned money as a seamstress. When Celeste was about eight, her father moved the family to Roosevelt, Long Island. Her parents divorced a few years later.

Celeste then went to work, lying about her age in order to secure a job at a nursing home to help her mother support the family. She graduated from Roosevelt High School in 1975 and shortly thereafter began working for Miss Black America. After she met Bobby, the two began dating.

"We just connected when we met," Celeste said. "But what do you know at 21?"

Bobby eventually rented a room in the Serrano home and began living with Celeste and her mother.

When Bobby met Celeste, he had three children by three different women. His first child, Indya, was born in 1975 when he played at FSU. Bobby and Indya's mother, Saundra Litman, married, but soon divorced.

"Part of my upbringing was, you get someone pregnant, you got to get married," Bobby said. "I wasn't thinking at the time I could just take care of my child." A few years later Bobby had another child, Robert Thomas, born in 1980 and out of wedlock to Patricia Thomas, an FSU student.

In 1977, his daughter Trae was born after he had a brief sexual encounter with her mother in Tallahassee. Bobby did not accept the fact that he fathered Trae until the two met for the first time in 2013. In all he had seven children by four women, and two were out of wedlock.

A few years after Bobby and Celeste met, she became pregnant with his child. The couple then bought a home of their own on Long Island. Their marriage was troubled from the beginning, he said.

"We started fighting from day one, but I cared enough for her to make the move," Bobby said. "I'll tell you something else. I knew I wasn't going to be true to that relationship."

Bobby and Celeste were married in March 1983. In August Celeste gave birth to their first child, Ashun.

Bobby and Celeste had three more children, Asia, Chante', and Tenisha. Celeste gave birth to four children within five and a half years. Bobby sometimes came home at three or four in the morning after partying with his teammates. There were other women, and lies about them to Celeste, early in their marriage.

*

Before Bobby and Celeste married, he met twenty-year-old Jacqueline Brown. She worked at the Garden of Eve, at a restaurant and bar in Hempstead, Long Island. Robert Miller introduced Bobby and Jacqueline.

Miller lived in Hempstead at the Hofstra County Estates and near where the Jets trained at Hofstra University. He worked for the city's Department of Public Works and met Bobby and other players at their training camp. Miller often had drinks with them after their practice sessions, he said.

"I just followed the team close back then," Miller said. "I liked going to their practices."

Miller and Bobby became friends during that period and remained so over the years. Miller married in 1985, with Bobby as his best man. Miller's nickname, Ichabod Crane, came from the tall character in the short story, "The Legend of Sleepy Hollow."

At six-foot four and 175 pounds, the nickname fit him. "Everybody just called him Ichabod," Bobby said.

Sometime after Bobby and Robert Miller met, he asked Bobby if he would ask the Jets' organization to give him a try-out. Miller played high school football, but not college ball.

The Jets agreed to the tryout but did not offer Miller a spot on the team.

"It didn't go too well," Miller said. "There were a lot of guys bigger and faster than me."

Miller met and had been around Jacqueline a few times at the Garden of Eve and had been struck by her radiant personality and beauty. Jacqueline, who Bobby would later refer to as "Jackie," and Miller considered each other friends. Jackie, a Native American, had dark hair, dark eyes, and brown skin.

Miller said he wanted Bobby to meet the "nice and hard-working" Jackie, and maybe the two would enjoy being around one another.

Bobby met Jackie during the summer of 1981 when Miller took him to the bar. Although Bobby had been in New York since '78, his rookie season with the Jets, Miller told Jackie he had just arrived from Georgia and did not know anyone and hoped she could help him feel welcomed.

Miller did not tell Jackie that Bobby played for the New York Jets. She responded to the introduction by giving Bobby a hug, a kiss on the cheek, and welcoming him to New York.

"I remember that kiss and hug to this day," Bobby said.

They were attracted to each other from the beginning. They talked that night, but not long, as other customers began to arrive. Bobby said he was smitten. He became attracted not only to her beauty, but also to her independent way of thinking and talking. And the confidence in which she carried herself.

"There was just something about him," Jackie said. "I remember he had these little flip-up sunglasses on when I met him."

She found him not only good-looking, but also easy mannered, with a disarming smile. Bobby, following Miller's lead, did not tell Jackie that night that he played for the Jets. If he had, that might have stopped their relationship before it even started.

Jackie had once dated a young man out of high school who, after playing college football, eventually went on to play for the San Diego Chargers. As that young man climbed the football ranks his attitude became self-centered and arrogant, she said. After that relationship ended, she told herself she would never again date another athlete — particularly football players. In fact, it was well known by customers, some of whom were other Jet's players, that she would not date either customers or athletes.

Not long after they met, Bobby and his Karate instructor were driving in Bobby's car when they passed Jackie who was walking with her sister. He pulled a u-turn and crossed to the other side of the road, pulling his car directly up to where the two women were walking. "He almost ran me over when he saw me," she said. His car stopped within one foot of her. "I saw he was excited when he drove up to me." Bobby asked Jackie for her phone number and after some prodding by her sister, she gave it him. He would later call her for a date — she accepted.

When he arrived at her home for the date, he handed her something she didn't expect and didn't want. It was an eight-by-ten autographed picture of himself in the Jet's uniform. She felt tricked and a little angry, she said. She did not want to date an athlete, particularly a professional football player, and now she didn't want to go out with Bobby. However, instead of backing out of the date, it turned out to be a double date with his cousin and his date, she decided to go through with the evening and planned not go out with him again.

They shared stories about growing up. Jackie learned about Bobby's childhood in the housing projects in Albany. A boyhood with few frills but with lots of love from friends and family. He told her about his strong and loving grandmother, and a father who he respected.

As the night moved on, Jackie did not think about Bobby the NFL player, but Bobby the kindred spirit, she said. Jackie's upbringing, although far away in distance, seemed to have similarities to Bobby's.

"I knew I loved him that day," she said.

Jackie was born in 1961 in Rapid City, South Dakota. Her maternal side is full Hunkpapa Lakota (Sioux) and her father's side is of Native and mixed origin. From her maternal lineage, she is a sixth generation descendant of Sitting Bull, one of the most revered nineteenth-century leaders of the Hunkpapa Lakota — of the Sioux Nation.

Jackie grew up steeped in her culture with a deep respect and appreciation for the spiritual lessons and laws that govern her today, the stories of Sitting Bull and One Bull and the spiritual influence Sitting Bull had, and still has, on her people. Since her childhood, she has always sought to honor and respect her lineage to One Bull and Sitting Bull, knowing that spirituality is the strength by which her family continues today. But over the years, how she viewed her responsibility as a descendant of Sitting Bull has changed.

"I used to think I spoke for all Indians when I opened my mouth," Jackie said. "As I got older I realized it was not my responsibility to speak for every Native American in North America." All people in all cultures must find their own ways, she said.

Sitting Bull, or Tatanka-Iyotnaka, born around 1831, was the last chief of the Hunkpapa Lakota and spiritual leader of the entire Sioux Nation, which spanned the greater Midwest region up into Canada. He defeated General George Custer at the Battle of the Little Big Horn and was the last leader to surrender his people, even unto is death, to the welfare of the federal government. In the book, *God is Red: A Native View of Religion,* published in 1994 by Vine Deloria, Jr., Sitting Bull's response to the question was:

Because I am a red man. If the Great Spirit had desired me to be a white man he would have made me so in the first place. He put in your heart certain wishes and plans, in my heart he put other and different desires. Each man is good in his sight. It is not necessary for eagles to be crows.

Bobby fell in love with Jackie, and in the early 1980s invited her to Albany, Georgia, to show her where he had grown up, and to meet his grandmother, Rebecca Jackson and other people important to him. Bobby liked the fact that Jackie was unimpressed with his professional football status. She became attracted to him for other reasons, the right reasons, he said.

In Albany she met Bobby's friends and family, including his daughter Indya. Bobby drove Jackie through the city, meeting people from his youth and showing her where he played sandlot football as a boy. Albany reminded her of Rapid City and growing up at Standing Rock Reservation, places where people were friendly and she was welcomed, she said. The trip confirmed that her and Bobby were indeed "kindred spirits."

*

Around the time Celeste Serrano told Bobby she was pregnant with his child, Jackie became pregnant with Bobby's child, but did not tell him. Jackie made a decision to have an abortion and didn't tell Bobby about it until sometime later.

"I wouldn't have agreed to marry Celeste if I had known Jackie was pregnant," Bobby said. "My heart back then said Jackie was the woman for me."

Bobby told Jackie he and Celeste were to marry. It would be almost twenty years before Bobby and Jackie reunited.

Bobby and Celeste got married March 20, 1983, on Long Island, but the day before the wedding he was arrested in Atlantic City, New Jersey. With Celeste pregnant, Bobby felt "pressured" into marrying her and decided to party with a couple of friends in Atlantic City before the wedding.

"I just wanted to get away for a few days and not think about the future," he said.

That's where his trouble began.

Sometime before his trip, Bobby bought a new BMW 320 with license plates that read, BOJACK, his nickname from his FSU days. He drove the vehicle to Atlantic City with his friends. In the car's trunk was a .357 magnum loaded with hollow point bullets.

He bought the weapon legally in Florida while there visiting his brothers. Possession of the gun was illegal in New York, he said.

"It was the Dirty Harry style," Bobby said. "I bought it not so much for protection but just to show off." Dirty Harry, a movie character played by Clint Eastwood, used the same kind of gun to kill criminals.

At Atlantic City, Bobby and his friends spent a few days drinking and gambling. They saw a boxing match. They smoked marijuana and snorted cocaine. On March 19 he planned to return to Long Island to attend his rehearsal dinner before the wedding.

Around mid-day, as Bobby drove the BMW on the Garden State Highway, a car drove up next to him with two white men inside.

"One of the white guys was wearing a T-shirt that had a Confederate flag on it," Bobby said. "Then the guy turned his chest toward us and pointed to the flag."

High on marijuana at the time, Bobby became angry and pulled his car off the road and stopped. He got out of the car, opened the trunk, and removed the .357 magnum.

"I was pissed at that guy and his flag," Bobby said. "I was stoned and didn't want to get married. But I should've left my gun in the car. I made some mistakes on that trip."

Bobby got back into his car with his gun, drove again onto the highway and eventually caught up to the vehicle with the two white guys, one wearing the Confederate flag. As Bobby approached their vehicle, he showed them, but didn't point directly at them, his gun, he said. After seeing the gun, the men in the other vehicle sped away and later notified the police that someone had pointed a gun at them.

A few minutes later, Bobby and his friends drove through and paid at a tollbooth. Moments later they were pulled over by two New Jersey State troopers.

"I tried to get out of my car," Bobby said. "But one had a shotgun on us and the other a pistol."

Three sets of hands then went through the BMW's sunroof. The troopers ordered Bobby and his friends out of the car, searched it, and found the gun and a small amount of marijuana. They did not find the cocaine hidden in a medicine container.

The three were then driven to a New Jersey State Police satellite holding area and handcuffed to a bench. Bobby told the troopers the gun and marijuana belonged to him, in an attempt to protect his friends from criminal charges, he said.

After several minutes of questioning and looking at their driver's licenses, one of the troopers asked Bobby and his two friends which one of them played for the New York Jets, which one was Bobby Jackson. Bobby told the trooper he played for the Jets, but the trooper became incredulous, telling Bobby he was too small to play in the NFL.

Charged with possession of less than an ounce of marijuana and possession of an illegal firearm, Bobby paid seven hundred dollars bail. He pled guilty to the first and only arrest in his life.

"I cooperated with them and was given probation," he said. "Every month for about a year, I had to meet with my probation officer but mostly we just talked football."

The media never learned of or reported the arrest, Bobby said. He made a big mistake that day, but it wouldn't be his last.

*

When Bobby retired from the NFL in 1986, he became distraught because injuries to his neck and legs had shortened his career. He had hoped to play longer and accomplish more on the field, including a Super Bowl victory.

"We were one game away from it in '82," Bobby said. "That still hurts even today when I think long about it."

Retirement became a difficult transition for Bobby. It did not begin well.

For almost a year after he left the NFL, he had affairs with other women, drank a lot, and used drugs. He didn't work, nor did he make much of an effort to find employment. For the first time in his adult life, without the challenge and satisfaction of football, he became adrift. At times the drug use and drinking became heavy.

"I was trying to replace the feeling of companionship and camaraderie from football that I had lost," Bobby said. "I got depressed. All of a sudden, you're made to feel like a has-been. I didn't handle the situation well."

His marriage to Celeste remained intact but sometimes in name only. Following the birth of their first child, Ashun in 1983, the couple had three more children. Asia born in '84 followed by Tenisha three years later, and finally Chante' in '88.

Around the end of 1987, Bobby was running out of the money he had saved from playing football. He signed his first professional contract with the Jets in 1978 for an annual salary of thirty thousand, with a signing bonus of eleven thousand. The most he ever made in one year, by the early '80s, was two hundred twenty-five thousand. His money woes worsened because of failed financial investments in real estate and oil, he said.

By the late 1980s, Bobby made a decision to do something more than use drugs and be with other women. Broke financially, if not emotionally, he said he needed a new direction in his life.

Former teammate, Burgess Owens, offered Bobby an opportunity to begin his own Amway business, and he accepted. Bobby and Celeste worked together in the business for a few years, selling health, beauty, and home care products. The couple often traveled together, and their relationship grew stronger during this period, Bobby said.

His drinking and drug use had moderated, but he still occasionally spent time with other women. The Amway business gave way to other jobs, including working as a sales representative for Word Perfect selling computer software in the early 1990s. Still, there were financial problems for Bobby and Celeste, and the couple declared bankruptcy in 2000.

In the late 1990s Bobby, who had stayed close to the Jets since his retirement, became the celebrity host for a home game when he met Howard Lippe, a representative with Modell's Sporting Goods. Modell's, founded in 1889, and today is the oldest family-owned and operated retail sporting goods store in the country. It's located in the Northeast and includes more than 150 stores.

"When I met Lippe at that game, I told him I was interested in working for his company," Bobby said. "He said he would give me an interview."

The interview went well, and Bobby took and passed a drug test before he began working with the company. "I had stopped smoking marijuana about six months before that. I was trying to clean my life up."

There were, however, long periods in his post-football life when Bobby referred to himself as a "functional addict" in his use of marijuana and cocaine.

"I didn't think I had a problem," he said. "I still got up and went to work. Was I an addict? I guess I was."

Since he retired from the NFL, working at Modell's has been Bobby's longest tenure with any job. He spent nearly twenty years with the company and became a regional marketing manager and community ambassador connected with eighteen stores in and around New York City. Part of his job included speaking at schools and warning students of the dangers of using drugs.

"I had been a hypocrite over the years by telling kids not to use drugs when I was using them myself," he said. "That's something I'm not proud of."

CHAPTER 11

The early part of the 2000s represented a difficult period for Bobby. His beloved grandmother, Rebecca Jackson, the woman who reared him in Albany, Georgia, died in December 2003. And his father Robert Charles Jackson, Sr., had suffered with cancer during that period and died September 2004. Both had been important and influential people in his life.

There had been periods in his marriage with Celeste in which the couple had grown closer, but Bobby longed for something else.

Jackie had married in 1988, she and her husband giving birth to a child and adopting others. Although it was, by all accounts, a fruitful and successful marriage, that perfect union ended in divorce in early 2004.

It was September 2004 when Jackie received a phone call from a mutual friend informing her that Bobby's father was dying from cancer and that Bobby was awaiting a flight to Georgia at LaGuardia Airport. Bobby had always experienced major anxiety flying commercial airlines and preferred to drive. Knowing that his father's passing was imminent; he was white knuckling the flight to afford him extra time with his father.

Bobby said he always admired his father, who had served in the Army, worked for years as a custodian, and had a beautiful singing voice. The divorce between his mother and father had caused pain for Bobby, as it would any child.

In his mind remained the image from his childhood after the divorce, when he saw his parents holding hands and hoped they would reunite and his family become whole again. And his hope never realized.

When Bobby saw his father for the last time, he returned to his childhood neighborhood driving slowly through the old streets. He saw the fields near Pine Avenue and the public housing projects where he played pick-up football games, raced the garbage trucks, and slept under the stars and dreamed of things to come.

He visited where he and his cousin Charlie Johnson and other neighborhood boys played games and talked about girls. There he first earned a reputation of a fast and fearless athlete, regardless of his size. The memories, both good and bad, came rushing back to him as he drove the streets of Albany during that trip home, with his father dying of cancer.

Jackie arrived at the airport that day in 2004 wanting to see him before he boarded the plane. This would be the last time she saw him as his father's son, and it was important. Bobby wore long basketball shorts, he looked gaunt, and not the muscle-toned figure Jackie expected to see. "He looked defeated on a lot of fronts," Jackie said. They hugged. "It was as if no time had passed between us."

The two spent more than an hour together at LaGuardia Airport talking about their children, their lives, and what the future might bring. Jackie's life was stressful following her divorce as she owned and operated an independent film company that she told Bobby she was in the process of closing down. She had recently suffered a minor stroke but did not tell Bobby about it at their meeting. She gave him some Xanax medication to help calm him before his flight. He took the pills and her phone number and boarded his flight.

He regularly telephoned Jackie, talking to her about his life. He said her voice gave him comfort and he wanted to spend time with her when he returned to New York. Although she wanted to see him, it was not good timing as she was trying to heal, going to physical therapy, and wasn't happy.

Once he returned to New York, their telephone calls graduated to monthly lunch or dinners where much was discussed and their friendship grew again. These were the "sounding board and non-judgmental conversations of two friends," she said. Although there was nothing intimated between the two Bobby felt a strong attraction to her, but Jackie remained cautious about a deeper relationship with him. Sometimes Bobby came to her apartment to sleep, and sometimes Jackie would hear him crying over the deaths of his grandmother and his father, she said.

Then it happened. One day in 2005, Jackie returned to her apartment, after a two-week absence, to a message on her answering machine from Bobby's wife. In the message, Celeste said she knew Bobby was seeing Jackie and that she should stay away from him. "I knew then, he was available," Jackie said. "That's just not the words of a jealous wife." After that message, Jackie began to think seriously about allowing Bobby back into her life but wasn't sure she cared about him the way she had twenty years earlier.

In 2005, Jackie bought a house on Long Island where she and her children could live. At the time, Bobby was still living in Long Island with his family. Jackie's house needed renovations and Bobby became involved in helping her find contractors who could do the work for her. Bobby began pushing hard for a full relationship with Jackie, she said. And the feelings she once had for him many years prior began to re-emerge.

Soon Jackie began to notice something different about Bobby. Something destructive. Bobby lost his temper quickly, his voice became loud, and he'd lose control of the simplest of situations. He became unpredictable and erratic for seemingly no apparent or logical reason, Jackie said.

Bobby's drug use, including crack, had gotten heavy by the end of 2005 and early 2006. Because of his often erratic and bizarre behavior, Jackie began to push him away hoping he would leave her alone, she said.

"I was trying to break off the relationship," she said. "Because things eventually got so bad."

He would show up uninvited at Jackie's house asking a series of questions in an animated way, displaying extreme behavior. Jackie initially didn't understand the cause of his strange behavior. However, eventually he would tell her about his drug problem, yet underreporting the depth of it.

This began Bobby's most destructive period of drug use. Up to that point, his cocaine use had been powder only, but he was introduced to crack cocaine by a woman he met. Bobby became both an addict and small-time drug dealer. He sometimes made a thousand dollars a week selling drugs, he said.

"I sold it when I had a lot of it," Bobby said. "But mainly I was a user. A heavy user for a while. I made some money but never kept it long."

Bobby's wife knew he was not only using, but selling as well. Some weekends from 2006 through 2008 he never left his house. He smoked his time away with crack cocaine and stayed stoned. He called himself a "zombie" during this period.

He tried to hide his drug use and selling from his children, and it worked for a while. Eventually they would know the truth, too. Most family members and friends in Georgia and elsewhere did not know how far he had fallen. Had they, they would've been shocked.

His behavior led to arguments with Jackie who reported him to the police, least once, to remove him from her property. Their relationship deteriorated and became tenuous at best. Jackie could not bring herself to turn her back on Bobby, especially after consulting his mother about his drug use, but refused to entertain his destructive behavior. This led her to place an electronic tracking device in his vehicle. "I wanted him to leave me alone, but I was always afraid something bad was going to happen to him back then," she said.

The ensuing season (beginning with Labor Day Weekend) would see Jackie confronting Bobby with other women at crack hotels when he was supposed to be out of town. And in the end, forcing him to face the fragmented person he had become, she removed the tracker from his car.

*

Jackie was taking her daughter's friend to MacArthur Airport at five in the morning to catch a flight back to Florida. Her daughter's friend noticed the "BOJACK" plates on the Chevy Impala that was in the bank drive thru. After a quick drop off Jackie followed Bobby, worried about what he was doing that time of morning.

Bobby had received a call that morning from the same girl Jackie had seen him with at the hotels over the Labor Day Weekend. She told Bobby she wanted some cocaine, he said. She wanted to party and said she would dance naked for him if he came with the drugs. He had the drugs and drove to a house where the woman lived with a roommate.

That morning, unlike other times Bobby drove his car during his drug-days, he did not have a gun in his vehicle. He had forgotten to take one. Sometimes he would drive with a .357 magnum in his car, and once he even kept an assault rifle in his car, an AK-47.

"I'm sure I was in some bad situations back then," Bobby said. "I didn't think about how dangerous they were. I did some pretty stupid things during that time."

Bobby drove onto a country road that morning and then to a "somewhat isolated area" known for crime and drug dealing, he said. He got out of his car and carried cocaine into a house where the woman was waiting. They used the drug, and she danced naked for him.

"This was a place where you could find skinheads," Jackie said, referring to the white racist group. "You could get hurt or killed where Bobby went that morning." Jackie followed Bobby to the house.

She stopped, parked her car, and walked to the front door. She knocked on the door and waited. Bobby heard the knock and thought it was the girl's boyfriend, he said. He figured he better get out of the house before the jealous boyfriend came in and found him and the girl together. He knocked the screen out of a window and prepared to jump out of it, but he saw Jackie looking at him.

"I thought then, 'How in the hell did she know I was here?' " Bobby said.

After some time, Bobby appeared at the door and Jackie convinced him to walk with her to the yard where she confronted him again about his dangerous behavior, about the drug use, about all the lies he had been telling her and everyone else. Bobby had told her, prior to that morning, he was no longer using drugs. That he had changed his life for the better. All lies.

Jackie told Bobby she had called the police and they were on their way. She told him she reported the drug use in the house and, furious, she told him she was going to hit him. She said she "didn't throw sucker punches and wanted him to know it was coming."

"I didn't hit back," Bobby said. "I was just trying to protect my face. I was in the wrong."

Then two police officers arrived. Bobby told the police Jackie had hit him and they asked him if he wanted to press criminal charges against her. He said no. The police made no arrest that morning and left the house after helping Jackie find her car keys she had dropped when she had hit Bobby.

"I was shaking when I left there," she said. "I wasn't angry, I was destroyed. He was a liar and was always going to be a liar. That was what I was thinking."

Jackie had had enough of the lies and drugs. Weeks went by and they said little to one another. Bobby made a few phone calls to her and wrote her a couple of letters. She received some e-mails from some of Bobby's children, one calling her "a crack-whore," claiming she used drugs with her father and blaming her for Bobby's troubles.

"That simply wasn't true," she said. "I didn't use drugs then or now."

He began to talk more and more about his drug habit and how he wanted to end it. How he wanted to make things better for himself and for the two of them. The more he talked about his problem and his willingness to address it, the more she came to believe that he would find a way to end his habit.

The two had always been good friends. To Jackie, not helping Bobby would be comparable to refusing to help a close friend. She talked to Bobby about seeing a professional counselor. He needed to be in a residential treatment center, maybe for a few months or so. Maybe that would be the beginning of a better way to live, she said.

"She wanted me then to get treatment," Bobby said. "I thought about it. She was right. I needed help and had to do something."

She drove Bobby by Seafield Center in Westhampton Beach on Long Island and suggested he consider being admitted to such a place in order to overcome his addiction. Seafield provides inpatient/outpatient treatment for addicts. They talked about it and Bobby decided against it. He told himself he would find another way to beat the "demons" within, he said.

CHAPTER 12

Bobby Jackson, the well-behaved boy from in Albany, Georgia, who once raced garbage trucks and later excited Jets' fans at Shea Stadium with his outstanding football play, had made his life hellish.

His drug addiction affected his work at Modell's Sporting Goods, where he was nearly fired because he missed several days at work, and when he was there, his work was often sloppy.

It became difficult for him to both understand and accept that he, whose athletic career became marked by great determination and self-discipline, had lost control of his own life. He had won many battles on the football field but for now he had lost the battle with drugs.

Finally, Jackie gave Bobby an ultimatum to either stop using drugs, entirely, or any relationship/friendship they had left would end for good. Still using drugs into 2009, he searched for salvation away from them.

"Crack cocaine was hard for me to beat," Bobby said. "The first time I smoked crack, it gave me a high like I never had before. I wanted more of it after that."

Each time after the first time, he chased but never matched that initial high. He had made a mess of things and didn't know how to fix them.

As the year passed, Bobby made a decision to end his drug use and the dangerous life he was living. He planned to do it on his own and without professional treatment. Motivation came through his longing to keep his relationship with Jackie intact and not to disappoint his children, family, and friends who watched him come of age in the housing projects in Georgia and to become an outstanding NFL player. People who respected him and needed his support and love.

"The thought in my mind then was, what would my kids think of me if it came out in the papers that I had been arrested and was going to jail?" Bobby said.

If he had been arrested or hurt in a drug deal, it would've surprised a lot of people, including many in Georgia, such as former coaches, teammates, and folks who followed his career from the beginning. Most of them were unaware of the kind of life he had been living during that period in New York.

In 2009 Jackie asked him to go with her to South Dakota and attend the sacred Lakota Sun Dance. This traditional ceremony of spiritual and healing powers Bobby knew little of, but it ultimately had a lasting impact on his life.

*

By the summer of 2009 Bobby began to turn away from the drugs that had both controlled him and endangered his life for the past few years. He did this on his own and with Jackie's help and encouragement and without going to a rehabilitation clinic or outpatient therapy. And he agreed that summer to drive with Jackie, nearly two thousand miles, to Standing Rock Reservation in South Dakota to attend the annual religious ceremony at the Sitting Bull Sun Dance Camp.

The annual campsite for Sun Dance sits on the same area in which the nineteenth century Lakota leader Sitting Bull grew up. The land remains sacred to the Lakota. The camp is located in northern South Dakota, an area of hills and endless stretches of prairie.

Any understanding of the Lakota culture must include its traditional and sacred reliance on the American Bison.

In the nineteenth century millions of these majestic animals roamed freely over the Great Plains. They were almost slaughtered into extinction by the late 1800s in efforts by the U. S. government to destroy Lakota culture.

Bobby traveled with Jackie that summer to see up close where she had grown up and to have a better understanding of the Lakota people, he said. Standing Rock was created by the government in 1868 following the Fort Laramie Treaty during the wars in which the Lakota were ultimately defeated and much of their ancestral lands taken from them.

Initially the reservation, which includes parts of both South and North Dakota, covered about 2.7 million acres. After further land confiscation by the government, today it includes about one million acres with a tribal enrollment of about 9,000, according to the Bureau of Indian Affairs, the federal agency in charge of overseeing Indian reservations.

In June of 2014 President Obama visited Standing Rock and said poverty and high school dropout rates among Native Americans should be "a moral call to action."

The 2010 U.S. census indicated that about 5.2 million people, 1.7 percent of the total U.S. population, identify as Native Americans or Alaska Native. Identifying themselves as Lakota or Sioux were 170,110 people. The largest tribal group was the Cherokee, with 809,105.

The federal poverty rate at Standing Rock was around forty-three percent, compared to about fifteen percent for the entire country. Fourteen percent of all Americans today do not have a high school diploma, but it is nineteen percent at Standing Rock. Fifteen percent of those living at Standing Rock have a bachelor's degree or higher. That number doubles for the entire country.

Bobby's hometown of Albany for the last several years has been one of the poorest cities in the nation, according to government statistics.

As of 2010, Albany's population was around 78,000 with about 27 percent living below the poverty line, much higher than the national average, but not as dramatic as Standing Rock. Bobby recognized the similarities the first time he visited Standing Rock in the summer of 2009 to watch the Sun Dance.

"Both places have a lot of poor people," Bobby said. "They remind you how hard it is for a lot of people in our country today."

*

In the book, *The Lance and the Shield: The Life and Times of Sitting Bull,* by Robert M. Utley and published in 1993, a thorough overview of the Sun Dance is provided which includes these lines:

> The sun dance was to the tribe what the vision quest was to the individual – a great outpouring of religious devotion and supplication aimed at securing tribal power and well-being. The sun dance honored and celebrated *Wi*, the sun, the all-powerful deity that reigned over the natural world, the underworld, and the spirit world, defender of the four cardinal virtues of bravery, fortitude, generosity, and wisdom. As it brought most of the bands together in tribal conclave, moreover, the sun dance afforded an occasion for visits, feasts, frolics, and all-around good times.

Utley describes in vivid detail a Sun Dance in the summer of 1875 in which the great leader Sitting Bull participated. One of Sitting Bull's purposes during this dance was to forge a bond between the Lakota band known as Hunkpapas and the Northern Cheyenne. He sought to form an alliance between these two groups to fight the U.S. Army, and others attempting to take their lands. Here's how Utley tells it:

> After the Sun-Dance lodge had been raised, Sitting Bull performed a special dance, full of holy symbolism and resonating with the themes of intertribal unity and triumphant

conquest. It represented Sitting Bull at the peak of his political, military, and spiritual powers.

Sitting Bull approached the Sun-Dance lodge astride a magnificent black war horse Ice (a holy man) had presented to him. Jagged streaks of white clay ran from the animal's rump down the right hip and leg, and from the root of each ear to the corners of the mouth. From the shoulders back to the rider's legs clustered white dots, representing hail.

Clad only in breechcloth, moccasins, and war bonnet, Sitting Bull was painted over his entire body with brilliant yellow clay. Black paint covered the lower half of his face, supporting a broad black streak that touched the corners of his eyes and ran across the forehead. Black bands circled his wrists and ankles. A round black disk on his chest represented the sun, a black crescent on this right shoulder blade the moon.

Dismounting but leading his horse, Sitting Bull danced into the lodge and around the circle to the back, then forward to the center pole and back to the rear. He called out, "I wish my friends to fill one pipe and I wish my people to fill one pipe."

This meant that the Cheyennes and Hunkpapas should fill pipes and smoke together in token of a pledge to act together. Black Crane, a Cheyenne, filled one pipe, a Hunkpapa another. Sitting Bull took Black Crane's pipe in his right hand and the Hunkpapa's in his left and motioned each to stand beside him. While the people in the lodge sang, Sitting Bull extended the two pipes toward the pole and, still holding his horse, danced forward to the pole, then back to the rear, the horse following. This he repeated several times as he made motions representing an approach on an enemy.

After the government defeated the Lakota and other tribes of the Plains by the late 1800s and confined most Indians to the reservation system, the Sun Dance became outlawed. But Native Americans continued to conduct the ritual secretly and under threat of arrest by government officials. Many whites, certainly many of those in positions of political power, viewed the Sun Dance as a pagan or barbaric ritual in opposition to Christian values.

Some said the ritual was tortuous and should be banned based on humanitarian reasons. The prevailing view of whites during the 1800s and into the following century supported policies to "Americanize Native Peoples" by replacing — destroying — native culture with white culture.

By the second part of the 1900s, fueled by the successful Civil Rights Movement for African Americans, national political leaders began to change their views on native cultures as well. Congress passed the Indian Religious Freedom Act of 1978, and it was signed into law by President Jimmy Carter, giving Native Americans the right once again to practice their traditional religious ceremonies.

*

As Bobby struggled to defeat his mental demons and crack cocaine around 2007 and 2008 Jackie endured physical and psychological challenges of her own. In 2006, she had jumped a fence, a stunt she has done dozens of times before, in order to watch Bobby coach young football players attending a camp.

As Jackie attempted to jump the fence, she suffered a full blow out to her left knee requiring re-constructive ACL surgery. After some time, following the surgery, it was discovered she had contracted hepatitis C, likely during her surgery. Her recovery grew painful and complicated, and included more than a year of chemotherapy treatments.

Not yet strong enough to participate in the Sun Dance Ceremony the summer of 2009 because dancers are not allowed food and water during the exhausting four days of dancing; Jackie planned to return to the reservation to give thanks for her recovery. While at the Sundance ceremony, Bobby and Jackie camped for a week in a tipi made of canvas brought to the campgrounds by one of Jackie's brothers.

At Sun Dance Camp that summer, Jackie offered prayers of thanks for her healing at the foot of the sacred cottonwood tree used in the ceremony, she said. She prayed at the tree, burning sage and covering her body in smoke as was practiced many years ago by the Lakota. These sacred rites were part of her upbringing on the reservation.

"I knew I was going to that tree," Jackie said. "A lot of people go to the tree to say thank you."

This symbolic form of purification at the sacred cottonwood tree Bobby saw for the first the first time at Standing Rock Reservation that summer.

He watched the dancers with respect and awe. He spoke with Lakota elders and learned aspects of their culture that stirred his imagination. About two hundred people attended the ceremony. Bobby helped during the week-long event by being part of the group that carried the cottonwood tree used in the ceremony, gathering firewood, and doing other things asked of him.

Campfires burn the entire time of the Sun Dance. Bobby added wood throughout the days. Prayer sticks were removed by those sitting around the fires and giving thanks for the gifts of the natural world.

There were periods of reflection at Sun Dance in which Bobby realized the Lakota culture could help him regain control of his life and finally stop using drugs, he said. He found a sense of beauty and peace in a place he didn't expect to find it. He heard the sounds of the drums at sunrise, saw the singing and dancing in the moonlight, and looked intently at the participants who had endured the challenges of the Sun Dance that summer. He saw about thirty dancers. Some had their skin pierced but did not scream in pain.

When he saw the dancers begin the ceremony, his thoughts went to a 1970s movie, *A Man Called Horse.* In the movie a white man willingly endures painful Native American rituals.

At Sun Dance Bobby prayed for those dancing, that their suffering might be eased. He prayed for those he did not know, all part of the ceremony. And he prayed for his family members, both living and dead.

These physical and mental challenges of the Sun Dance appealed to Bobby. As he watched he felt compelled to become a dancer himself. He had a similar experience when he attended Carver Junior High School in Albany. As a member of the school's band, he traveled with other students to Atlanta to watch the Georgia Tech football team play the University of South Carolina.

He knew while watching that game that one day he'd play organized football. He said he knew watching the Sun Dance for the first time that one day he would become a dancer himself. It may be one of the pathways to a renewed life, he thought then.

Jackie watched Bobby as he watched the dancers endure their ordeals, and she recognized within him an admiration for those he was watching. With Jackie's encouragement, Bobby asked the holy men at Standing Rock if he could become a dancer the following summer, 2010. He told them he hoped through the Sun Dance to give thanks for the good things that had happened in his life, to honor his family members who had died, specifically his father and grandmother, and to gain strength from the ritual that would ultimately help him lead a better life. They agreed to allow Bobby to dance.

"It was just something I had to know if I could do," Bobby said. "At the time I was trying to overcome some personal demons. My life was beginning to get better then, and I wanted the challenge of the Sun Dance."

When they returned to Long Island, Bobby began preparation for the Sun Dance the following summer. He continued to stay away from drugs and did not drink excessively. He got in good physical shape with regular running and weight lifting, as he had trained years earlier when he played football. He even went long periods without food and water because there would be none of either during the dancing.

"There's really nothing you can do to train for it," Bobby said.

The incredible physical and mental discipline required would be unlike anything he had ever experienced in his life, he said. Football was tough, but not Sun Dance tough.

His relationship with Jackie improved during the year. He began to see things more clearly, important things such as love, family, and the willingness to live in truth. He became a better parent, freeing himself from crack cocaine and the dangerous lifestyle he had been living prior to the summer of 2009.

Going into the summer of 2010, he said, "I was focused. I wanted to see what my limitations were and stretch beyond that. You basically get to the point where all your resistance is gone and will power takes over. You must make yourself a willing participant."

CHAPTER 13

Because of the important religious meanings of the Sun Dance, the most sacred of the Lakota rituals, participants are forbidden to reveal all of what occurs during the ceremony. Bobby described to me some of the details of his first of four consecutive Sun Dances in the summer of 2010. But other details he would not speak of.

He made a commitment to the holy men that he would dance at the next four annual ceremonies. In Lakota culture four itself is a sacred number, indicating the four seasons, and the four cardinal directions. Three of the four times Bobby danced, he endured the painful ordeal of the piercing of the skin.

Each time he accepted the piercing, he did not cry out in pain or show any outward emotions, he said.

Bobby grew up attending a Baptist church in Albany at the insistence of his grandmother, Rebecca Jackson. Following his first visit to Standing Rock Reservation, the spiritual nourishment of his life came less from the inside of a church and more through aspects of the Lakota culture, he said.

When he danced in 2010, he wore a crown of sacred woven sage, braided sage around both ankles and both wrists, and he was barefooted and shirtless. He wore a pair of shorts covered by a skirt of light cloth. All dancers dressed this way, and all were given a whistle made of an eagle's bone to be blown throughout the dancing. Bobby and about thirty other dancers participated in the ceremony at Standing Rock Reservation that summer.

On each of the four days of dancing, drums were played before sunrise to signal the beginning of the ritual. With the sound of the drums, Bobby and the other dancers lined up single file, such as players do before a drill at football practice. Dancers kept the same assigned order each time they lined up, and were not to touch one another while in line. People gathered silently around the sacred circle and sacred cottonwood tree to watch and pay respect to the dancers. Campfires remained burning throughout the ceremony.

Before the start of the first day of dancing, participants were given a small amount of tea made with sage to drink. For the next four days they could not consume either food or water. Fasting leads to spiritual growth, according to many religious traditions, including the Lakota. But if it rained and rainwater filled their bowls, they were allowed to drink from them. This occurred once during Bobby's four years of dancing.

"That's all part of the mental challenge," Bobby said. "Not being able to eat or drink for four days. That takes a great deal of discipline."

Dancers await the rising sun. The ritual begins once the sun appears over the hills.

The dancing included constant movement, shuffling of the feet, high knee kicks, and hands being raised when dancers were instructed to do so by those who supervised and instructed them, Bobby said. He referred to those supervisors as "drill sergeants" because of their constant demands on the dancers. And as the dancers moved they were instructed to blow the eagle bone whistles that had been given to them.

"Sometimes it was just like running in place," Bobby said. "Once the dancing began, we never stopped."

The dancers were told that while they danced, they could only focus their eyes on two things. The sacred sun and the sacred cottonwood tree.

The sun beat upon the dancers as they constantly moved and blew the eagle bone whistle. Dancers were forbidden to look at those who were watching the ceremony. The dancing continued throughout the day, but dancers were given breaks in which they left the sacred circle for an hour or so.

During the breaks Bobby found a shady spot near a tipi, slept there and when the drums were played again he returned with the other participants ready to dance again. And during breaks and at night, dancers relieved themselves in outhouses constructed for the ceremony. When Bobby did so, he looked about for rattlesnakes. He didn't see any, but he knew they were out there, he said.

Dancers were not allowed to bathe or brush their teeth for four days. They could wipe themselves with a wet cloth to ease the heat and sweating. Dancers were living in a "natural state," Bobby said.

The dancing continued, with interspersed breaks each day, until the sun disappeared over the hills. When the sun was gone, so was the day's dancing. As the dancers methodically lined up to leave the sacred circle for the day, they did so with heads bowed, able to sometimes recognize the people who came to watch them by seeing their feet, Bobby said. He saw Jackie in this manner.

Bobby slept until the sound of the drums the following morning. Sleep came easy from the exhaustion of the dancing. He grew weak during his first Sun Dance and thought he couldn't finish the four-day ritual. He doubted himself. Sometimes that happened to participants unable to endure what they had initially accepted, and they would withdraw from the ceremony, he said. Bobby saw it happen all four times he danced.

But he refocused in 2010, thought more about honoring his father and grandmother by completing the ceremony, and related what he was experiencing to the demanding Graves Springs Football Camp he attended in South Georgia, he said.

At that two-week camp there were three practices a day and usually no water during practices. The Sun Dance required much more sacrifice from the individual than Graves Springs, but those memories gave Bobby strength to continue dancing.

"What helped me get through the dancing in 2010 was thinking back about my high school football camp and how tough that was," Bobby said.

During the ceremony, if a participant became weak and was not dancing with proper energy, those supervising the dancing took him/her to the sacred tree to pray. There they fanned him/her, cleaning that person with eagle feather fans. Most times this re-energized the dancer as he returned to the line.

For four days Bobby danced, with Jackie and other members of her family and the Lakota tribe watching him. He found the internal strength each day to continue, despite having no food and water, and hurting physically from the incisions in his chest. The old ways of the Lakota giving strength to those living in the modern world.

At sundown on the fourth and final day of the ceremony, the dancers eat a traditional meal that includes buffalo tongue and chokecherry juice. All the dancers conclude the ceremony together. Afterwards, Bobby had his fill of watermelon he had asked Jackie to provide for him. He slept and ate, and slept and ate some more, as his body recovered for the four days of dancing.

"Food never tasted so good," he said. "And water never tasted so good."

The sacrifice was worth it, he said. He had committed himself to four years of dancing, and he fulfilled that commitment in the summer of 2013. He did so through the blessings of the Lakota people and through the strength given to him from his father and grandmother, he said.

"People who loved you and cared for you are never really gone, even when they die," Bobby said. "I believe that even more, now that I've completed the Sun Dance."

After the 2010 Sun Dance, Bobby for the first time since he retired from the NFL in 1986, said he felt like he was part of something bigger then himself.

"It was all worth it," he said. "It made me feel part of a team again, and we won."

Jackie was not surprised that Bobby completed his four-year commitment to the Sun Dance, she said. She saw that Bobby admired those he saw dancing in 2009. That admiration led to inspiration within him to accept the physical and mental challenges of the Sun Dance. Bobby's willingness to not only learn about the Lakota culture, but become a direct participant in its most sacred religious ritual, led to the strengthening of their relationship, she said.

"I had every confidence in him that he was going to fulfill his commitment," Jackie said, "I was so proud of him when he did."

CHAPTER 14

When Ashun Jackson, Bobby and Celeste's first child, was about six, Bobby took him to the Police Athletic League so his son could race on a track with other boys. During Ashun's races on Long Island, Bobby realized his son had outstanding speed.

"I knew then that joker was fast," Bobby said. "I said to myself back then, 'He's got my speed.' And I turned out to be right."

Ashun grew up around professional football players with Bobby, who, after his retirement, often took his son to watch the Jets practice and play. Ashun befriended Wesley Walker, Bruce Harper, and others who were his father's teammates.

"I consider some of those guys my extended family today," Ashun said. "I learned a lot about football from watching those guys."

Bobby had Ashun in karate lessons when he was young, and he started playing organized football in middle school. Ashun graduated from Walt Whitman High School on Long Island in 2001, where he excelled at running back. Having a former outstanding NFL player for a father was a thought that barely left Ashun's mind when he played high school football with his dad in the stands watching.

Like his father he was not big at five-foot seven and only 145 pounds. He played big, though, and once ran a kickoff back for a 99-yard touchdown. There was no overt pressure from Bobby for Ashun to play and excel at football, Ashun said. But the attention Ashun received by being Bobby Jackson's son became something that he "thrived on."

After high school, Ashun accepted a scholarship to play football at nearby Hofstra University. There, coaches converted him to cornerback, but he wanted to play offense, he said. After two years at Hofstra and playing defense only, Ashun transferred to Tuskegee University in Alabama.

"I wanted to play wide receiver at Hofstra, but it just didn't work out that way," Ashun said.

Bobby supported Ashun's decision to transfer and play offense, something that he had wanted in some ways for himself throughout his collegiate and professional careers.

Ashun started at wide receiver for Tuskegee for two years and was part of the 2006 team that was declared co-champions of the Southern Intercollegiate Athletic Conference. They were awarded a share of the title with Albany State University after Miles College reported it had played an ineligible player and forfeited its victories, including one over Tuskegee.

Bobby attended a few of Ashun's games when he was with Tuskegee, where he earned a degree in sales and marketing in 2007. As of 2015 Ashun owned a personal training business on Long Island, primarily helping condition college football players.

During the summers when Ashun and his sisters were young, Bobby and their mother drove the family nearly a thousand miles from Long Island to Bobby's hometown of Albany. The family spent a couple of weeks there. They had a brown Astro van for some of these trips, and Bobby removed the middle seat, giving his children more room to stretch in the back as they headed south. These trips made a lasting impression on Ashun and his sisters.

"My dad basically grew up in a shack," Ashun said. "He wanted me and my sisters to know about his life. It was a very humble beginning."

Ashun saw where his father lived in the housing project, the neighborhoods he played in when he was a boy, and the alleys where he raced the garbage trucks. They met Bobby's friends, his high school teammates, and others who helped Bobby along the way.

They saw where their father went to high school, and the stadium he played in as an Albany High School Indian in the early 1970s.

The family usually stayed with Bobby's grandmother, Rebecca Jackson, in the house Bobby bought for her. While on the road, they listened to music and often sang together. Earth, Wind and Fire, a 1970s group, became a favorite of Bobby's, who had a good singing voice like his father before him, his children said. Bobby could hit the high notes of the songs as his children accompanied him as they traveled south, and then back to Long Island. These were fun family trips.

These were important trips to Bobby, not only because he spent time with his family, but he wanted his children to see and understand where and how he grew up. There were plenty of struggles, but there was plenty of love, too, he said.

Bobby's daughter Asia, born in 1984, looked forward to these summer trips and to experience the differences between Long Island and Albany.

The red clay, the Spanish moss hanging from giant oak trees that lined residential areas, and the often suffocating summer heat pitched her and her siblings in another world, the world of the deep south, she said.

Bobby's family and friends in Albany welcomed his children with openness and love, the children said. Bobby's children were covered in love from their great-grandmother, Rebecca Jackson, who they referred to as "Na." She loved them the way she had their father.

"We were always surrounded by love," Asia Jackson said. "I'll always remember Dad's big smiles when we took these trips. Going down there are some of my best memories from childhood."

Asia played few sports growing up but enjoyed playing music. She played both the violin and clarinet while a student at Walt Whitman High School. Her father attended her recitals, supporting her fully in the things that mattered to her, she said.

Through Bobby's periods drug use, affairs with women, and as his marriage to Asia's mother began to crumble, he remained a steady hand in the lives' of his children, she said.

"He did the best he could to keep everybody happy," Asia said. "He made sure my mother and his children had everything they needed."

Asia first came to realize her father's athletic achievements when he was inducted to the FSU Hall of Fame in the early 1990s. She had watched her two brothers play college football and saw how they, as well as some of their teammates, turned to Bobby for guidance. She saw them show great respect to her father for what he once was on the football field. And she learned what kind of player he had been in the NFL.

She traveled to West Africa once and described the trip as a "spiritual pilgrimage." Along the way she spoke with a photographer on the plane. She told the man who she was and who her father was. The man became visibly excited and told her that Bobby Jackson was one of his all-time favorite NFL players. Then he used his iPad and showed Asia a highlight film of her father playing for the Jets.

"I knew he had been a great football player," she said. "I remember how my brother and his friends all looked up to him. I'll never forget that day on the plane when I was going to Africa."

Today, Ashun is closer to his father than he was when he was a boy. "Back then I was probably closer to my mom," he said.

On November 9, 2014, Bobby represented the Jets as ceremonial game captain for the Jets-Steelers contest at Met Life

Stadium in East Rutherford, New Jersey. He asked his son Ashun to be with him that day.

Bobby led the Jets onto the field before the game, talked to the players and coaches, and participated in the coin toss before the opening kickoff. Going into the game, the Jets were 1-8 and the Steelers 5-4 and favored to beat New York. At the stadium, Bobby and Ashun had their pictures taken together and enjoyed the thrill of the game.

Watching the Jets play became a visible reminder to Bobby of all that he had accomplished on the football field at Albany High, FSU, and with Jets. The Jets surprised a lot of football fans that day and upset the Steelers 20-13.

"I was proud of them," Bobby said. "There had been a lot of trash talking from the Steelers' fans before the game. They were quiet when it was over."

Both Bobby and Ashun wore New York Jets' jerseys when the Jets beat the Steelers. "That was a good day for him," Ashun said. "We had a big time that day. I was excited to share that with him."

Those kinds of moments of recognition are important to Bobby, who in some ways still feels underappreciated for his contributions to the Jets, Ashun said.

"For most of his life my dad had a huge chip on his shoulders, and this is something I didn't understand until I got older," Ashun said. "He was always having to prove himself because of his size. Some people might think he's the meanest man in the world, but he's actually the most kind-hearted person I know. There were times in his life when he didn't know how to turn that meanness off. People did misconstrue his personality."

Bobby's past drug use and his affairs with other women while married to Ashun's mother do not lessen the respect and admiration he has for his father, Ashun said.

"Everyone has their issues," he said. "What matters is that you try to get better. My dad has made things better in his life the last few years. He's an awesome individual, and I try to be like him. He would like people to understand and remember his legacy as someone who did change his life."

*

Tenisha was born to Bobby and Celeste in 1987. She graduated from Walt Whitman High School in 2005, where she was a cheerleader and an excellent sprinter on the track team. She ran the 100-meter sprint and the 400-meter relay. Bobby helped her develop her speed by working with her on the track during weekends, and he watched her compete against other high school athletes. He taught her discipline, like he did all his children, but he could spoil her as well, she said.

She called herself "a daddy's girl," and said she was practically "attached to his ankle" when she was growing up. And she referred to him as a "fun dad."

Around midnight one Christmas night when she was young, her and her siblings heard a loud "*Ho! Ho! Ho!*" They got out of their beds to see their dad coming down the stairs dressed as Santa Claus. Then he tripped and fell, and his children laughed and laughed. Santa was unhurt.

Tenisha sometimes found it easy to trick her father and have him do what she wanted him to do. During sixth grade she did not like school, she said. She went through a few weeks when she asked her teacher if she could go to the school's office around noon on Friday. She faked being sick and school administrators called her dad. Bobby picked her up and school, and they'd spend the rest of the day together. Bobby finally told her not to call again unless she was actually sick.

"I used to get my dad to do almost anything," Tenisha said.

Her father used to take her to events sponsored by the New York Jets, still does occasionally, and people would approach him for his autograph and to have their pictures taken with him. They told him what an incredible football player he had been in the late 1970s and early '80s and how much they loved watching him, Tenisha said.

Bobby made two such appearances prior to the 2015 Super Bowl. When Tenisha went with her father to these events, she'd look and listen closely as people praised her father and the way he played the game. They talked about how hard he hit opponents and his supreme athleticism on the field. They talked about his commitment to team when the Jets were winning more than they were losing in the early 1980s.

"It's still inspirational," Tenisha said. "I often think about everything he has accomplished and how far he came in his life. He's still my role model. It never gets old thinking about it."

When she became an adult, she learned there were long periods in her father's life when he had been a heavy drug user. She never saw him do drugs. Never suspected it, because he was always there for her as a father, loving and caring for her and her siblings, she said.

Bobby hid his drug addiction from his children. But she heard the many arguments between her father and mother and realized there was much pain between them over the years, she said.

There were short periods of separation between her parents, but it wasn't until their youngest child, Chante', graduated from high school in 2006 that Bobby moved out of the family home for good.

I interviewed Tenisha around 2015 when she was living on Long Island and working for a non-profit, Mercy First, that works with troubled teens. Mercy First is one of New York's leading non-profit human service agencies. It has around five hundred employees serving about 3,200 children and their families regardless of race, religion, sexual orientation, or physical condition.

"My mother never bashed my father in front of us when there were problems," Tenisha said. "My dad was a great father."

Tenisha described her relationship with her stepmother Jackie as a "good one now," but years earlier she blamed Jackie for parent's divorce. She said, since then, she has always been respectful to Jackie. "I look at my dad today, and he's happy. That's what counts."

Bobby and Celeste divorced in 2013. But family trips to Albany and traveling with her parents when they sold Amway products, are fond memories for their youngest child Chante'. And she competed for Walt Whitman's track team in the 100-meter sprint and long jump.

"I had a super hero for a dad," she said.

Today Chante' has a child of her own and, together with her child, lives with her mother on Long Island. As of 2015 she worked for a nursing home providing care for the elderly. A few years ago, she lived with her father. Throughout her childhood and into adulthood, Chante' did not hear her father complain when there were personal struggles in his life. He took care of her and her siblings, and he would "always wear a smile," she said.

Looking back at her parent's marital troubles, separation, and finally divorce, Chante' still gets angry sometimes. But she spoke of both a strong and loving father, and a strong and loving mother. "I was fortunate to have both," she said.

But Jackie's relationship with her father is "always going to be a touchy subject," she said. There were times when Chante' held anger toward Jackie. That changed eventually.

"I got a chance to meet Jackie back then," she said. "I let her know what was on my mind. We came to an understanding. Jackie's a brilliant woman, and I guess my dad's happy."

CHAPTER 15

After the 1982 AFC championship game in Miami, a photograph was taken of two-year-old Robert Thomas with his father, Bobby, in the Jets' locker room. Robert was living in South Florida at the time with his mother, Patricia Thomas. Bobby had had a brief relationship with Patricia when she was living in Tallahassee.

Bobby had seen little of Robert Thomas since he was born, but his mother brought him to the game in Miami to see his father. Because of the rainy and windy weather, Robert Thomas had been covered from his shoulders down in a garbage bag, in an effort to keep him dry during the game.

"My most vivid memory with him when I was growing up is that picture of us after the game," Robert Thomas said.

By the time Robert Thomas began attending elementary school, he realized he was one of the fastest boys around.

"I never lost a race at school," he said.

By his sophomore year at Fort Pierce Westwood High School in Fort Pierce, Florida, he started as running back and did so until he graduated in 1998. He became a standout on the track team as well. Bobby never saw his son play high school football. During Robert Thomas's formative years, Bobby wrote an occasional letter and telephoned him periodically, Bobby said.

"It was more of a holiday type-thing," Robert Thomas said, when the two did actually see one another. But their relationship would change once Robert Thomas graduated from high school.

During one track meet Robert Thomas met a coach who asked him if he was interested in playing football at Hofstra

University on Long Island. At the time Robert knew little about Hofstra. He did not know the school was in Hempstead on Long Island, where his father lived.

"Where I was growing up it was all Florida State or the University of Florida," Robert Thomas said. "I didn't know anything about Hofstra."

Hofstra head coach Joe Gardi had been an assistant with the New York Jets when Bobby played for them. When Bobby found out Robert Thomas was interested in playing at Hofstra, he called Gardi, hoping to get his son to Long Island for a workout session. After Robert Thomas worked out at Hofstra, they offered a scholarship and he earned a starting position at cornerback about four games into his freshmen year in 1998.

Both of Bobby's sons, Robert Thomas and Ashun, played briefly together at Hofstra before Ashun transferred to Tuskegee University. Robert Thomas had an immediate impact on Hofstra's team. He became a starting cornerback for four years. During the 1999 regular season he had twenty solo and eighteen assisted tackles. The same year he had four interceptions, tied for the team lead. His best collegiate time in the forty-yard dash was 4.27 seconds, surpassing his dad's best at any level of competition.

"He was faster than me," Bobby said. "And he was just a lot of fun to watch."

In 1999, Hofstra finished 10-1 during the regular season and received the Lambert Cup as the top Division I-AA team in the East.

Robert Thomas had one of his best games as a junior on October 13, 2000, when he scored two touchdowns during a thirteen-second span when Hofstra beat Liberty University 42-14 in Hempstead. The first came on a punt return of 60 yards, and the second was from a 23 yard interception.

He came to Hofstra in the middle of Gardi's tenure there. Gardi took over the program in 1990, and by the time he retired in 2005, he recorded ten winning seasons and an overall record of 119-62-2. Hofstra ended its 72-year-old football program in 2009, when school officials cited the high cost of maintaining it, and waning interest among the school's fans.

With Robert Thomas playing football in Hempstead where his father lived, he and Bobby for the first time began to develop a father-son relationship. They spent time together, talking and enjoying each other's company. Bobby attended nearly all of his games, home and away. When they talked, much of it was about football.

On Sundays, Robert Thomas often visited his father's house reviewing game films with him and listening closely to everything he father said. These instructional sessions made him a better cornerback.

"His word was law," he said. "He told me little things that only a star NFL defensive back could teach you."

Robert Thomas wanted then what his father had had, he said. He wanted an opportunity to play in the NFL.

"If it weren't for him, I wouldn't have come close to reaching my potential," Robert Thomas said.

After his career at Hofstra ended, he signed as a free agent with the San Francisco 49ers, but injured his groin during camp and was released. Unlike his father, he would not play at the professional level.

"I always thought, and still do, that Robert could've played at the next level," Bobby said. "But it just didn't work out that way. He had great speed and was a great competitor. He was faster than me."

In 2003 Robert Thomas earned a degree at Hofstra in psychology, and as of 2015 was working for a recovery center for alcoholics and drug addicts in Fort Pierce, Florida. During the summers since he graduated from college, he is often in New York visiting his father.

Despite his separation from his father during his youth, he doesn't "hold any grudges" because of the past, he said.

"That's one of the things that my dad taught me," Robert Thomas said. "Everybody deserves a second chance and to take responsibility for their actions."

He didn't know the depths of his father's drug problems that began just a few years after he graduated from college. "He kept it away from his kids, but he never short-changed his kids," Robert Thomas said.

*

The first of Bobby's seven children, Indya Jackson, was born in 1975. She said she remembered her mother, Saundra Litman, struggling financially after her short marriage with Bobby ended in divorce. She spent her childhood mostly living with her mother but sometimes with her father. Around the second grade she moved to Long Island and lived with Bobby for a few years.

She saw the Jets play, made friends and went to house parties. While a student at Westbury Junior High School on Long Island, she became "popular" in school, with her dad a star for the Jets, Indya said.

But she had a difficult family life. "This blended family my dad created wasn't the best for me," she said. "Sometimes there was animosity. I didn't experience a happy childhood."

During her later teenage years, she returned to living with her mother in Georgia, and graduated from Waycross High School in 1994. Waycross is a two-hour drive east of Albany toward the Georgia coast. The years she was away from her father, she visited him during the summers and went on family trips with him.

On one trip with him to Florida to visit family in 2009, Indya overheard a conversation indicating her father had been using drugs. This surprised her, she said.

"At that time I didn't know what was going on," Indya said. "And I didn't hear from him that much back then."

She said she doesn't harshly judge her father for the years in which he used drugs and put his life in danger, and the years they were away from each other.

"That's life," she said. "Everybody goes through life. I've always been proud of his accomplishments. He grew up in the projects and had to overcome a lot of setbacks" when he was a boy.

In the end, she described her father as being "dependable, easy to talk to, and loving." Indya is not married and has a teenage daughter, Evani, one of Bobby's five grandchildren.

Indya earned a two-year nursing degree from Brevard Community College in Florida and as of 2015 was working on a four-year nursing degree from Farmingdale State College on Long Island, giving her and her father more opportunities to see one another.

"I get to see him all the time now," she said.

CHAPTER 16

In 2013 an administrator from Albany High School notified Bobby that his football number, 45, would be retired. A pre-game ceremony to honor him was scheduled for September 13. No other number in school history had been retired.

Bobby contacted friends and family and traveled to Albany as he had done many times since leaving Georgia in the early 1970s. The high school stadium he played in sits between the school he attended, and the housing projects where he once lived with his grandmother.

While in the stadium before the ceremony, he thought of the many times he played sandlot football with boys of the housing projects, raced the local garbage trucks, and played football as an Albany High Indian.

He thought of his dreams of being a pro football player. Dreams that were realized. And he thought of his family, coaches at Albany High School, and friends who helped him as he came of age as a young athlete in the 1970s.

That night he wore shorts, tennis shoes, T-shirt, and a cap, all usual attire for Bobby. His youthful appearance did not reflect a man in his mid-fifties. He could've passed as a newly-hired high school coach just out of college.

Family and friends, including his mother, stood behind Bobby, as the ceremony unfolded on the field before the game between Albany High and nearby Mitchell County High School. Albany High School lost the game 20-14.

And that night Bobby's former high school head coach, Ferrell Henry, spoke during the ceremony.

"Bobby earned this honor the right way," Henry said. "He earned it through hard work, sacrifice, and great self-discipline. And he had earned a reputation for his love of contact. Bobby had developed into possibly the best defensive back to wear the orange and green," school colors for Albany High School.

Henry spoke in detail of Bobby's work ethic in the weight room and how he changed his body from that of "a little ol' skinny fellow" to an imposing athlete who could outrun everyone else on a football field or at a track meet.

Bobby went from 135-pound sophomore to around 170 pounds by the time he graduated, Henry said.

And his relationship with Henry has been close since he played under him in the early 1970s. Henry was a "father-figure" then and still is, Bobby said.

Always the fair and tough disciplinarian, Henry, along with other coaches at Albany High School like defensive backfield coach Ronnie Archer and B-Team coach Willie Magwood, molded Bobby into the great collegiate and professional player he became. Henry and offensive back coach Phil Spooner, who had both played at FSU, promoted Bobby to the coaches there before he accepted the scholarship offer.

Bobby always appreciated that about Henry and others at Albany High, knowing they cared for him not just as an outstanding player, but as a young man who they wanted to see grow up and live a good and decent life. Henry coached every player the same way he did Bobby in terms of wanting them to grow successfully into manhood, Bobby said.

I can attest to that as well.

The values he taught on the football field such as hard work, helping one another, and the willingness to continue to fight and do your best when things become difficult, can all transfer beyond the field, Bobby said.

Bobby came to see his life in these terms because of what the coaches at Albany High School had instilled in him years ago. These values have sustained him during his most difficult times. And when he works today with young football players through Football University, what comes through him is what he learned from Henry and other coaches at Albany High School.

"I try to pass it all down to my own kids and to the young players I work with," Bobby said. "I've tried to teach them the same lessons I got from Coach Henry. In some ways it's about sharing with others. The things Coach Henry gave to me, I don't want to keep to myself."

In his efforts to end his drug habit, Bobby thought about how hurt and disappointed his former coaches would be if they knew what kind of life he had fallen into, he said. It hurt and embarrassed him just to think about what *they* would think had they known. His fear of disappointing Henry and others who he played under motivated him to begin to do the right thing, stop using cocaine, and restore his life. By 2009 he had done so and has stayed away from drugs, and that dangerous lifestyle, since then.

Before Henry finished speaking about Bobby that night in 2013, he reminded those at the stadium that Bobby's honors included being selected as one of the top three cornerbacks for the All-Time Jets Team and being inducted in the early 1990s in both the Florida State University Sports Hall of Fame and the Albany Sports Hall of Fame.

Bobby received a framed white number 45 jersey, a carved Indian statue, and a new letter jacket, having lost his several years earlier during a move. Bobby wore number 40 for both the FSU Seminoles and the New York Jets.

He told the crowd at the stadium, "Being the first player to get honored, I'll carry this with the highest respect." And he reminded them of this often-told story from his boyhood growing up in the nearby neighborhood, "And I was the only one to catch the trash truck and get a ride on it."

The *Albany Herald,* the local daily newspaper, reported the event, describing Bobby as "a ball hawk, a one-of-a-kind disrupter on defense. And on special teams? He was a blur." The story about Bobby referred to a FSU website dedicated to Seminole sports history.

> The 5'11', 185 lbs. speedster from Albany, GA, took little time dismantling all competition for the defensive back spot at Florida State. Soon after freshman Bobby Jackson set foot on the Seminole practice fields he claimed his starting position. Jackson's speed and quickness blended dangerously with an appetite for aggressive hitting. His excellent hands and an outstanding knack for covering receivers one-on-one made Jackson an immovable object in the defensive secondary.

All of what the above passage described was accurate except the part about being five-foot eleven and 185 pounds. As Bobby said, "Sometimes people stretched me."

Albany High School's athletic director Archie Chatmon presented the jersey and Indian statue to Bobby. Before the event he told the paper, "Yes, it's overdue. It's something we should've done a long time ago, and we've wanted to do for a while. It just finally happened to work out."

Chatmon is a few years younger than Bobby and attended Albany High School's crosstown rival Westover High School in the mid-1970s.

"We all followed him," Chatmon said. "He was a great, great player."

In the same story Bobby was quoted as saying the honor "feels very good, very satisfying." But Al Smith, a former basketball star at Albany High School in the early 1970s, should've been the first to have his number retired, Bobby said. Smith played basketball for both FSU and Jackson State before spending nearly eighteen years playing professionally overseas.

Later Bobby said of all the honors he has received through football, including both collegiate and professional, the most important to him was what he earned at Albany High School. In 1972 the local newspaper selected him as part of the All-City Defensive Team. Players were picked from the four public high schools. Then in 1973 he was selected as part of the All-City Offensive Team.

"To me that's more important than the All-Time Jets Team," he said, "and the FSU Hall of Fame. It was the first time I had ever been recognized, and it's what I'm most proud of."

*

That night at Hugh Mills Stadium, Bobby received something else, something more meaningful than a jersey encased in glass. Bobby met for the first time his daughter born in 1977.

Trae Leonard and her husband and three children live in Tallahassee. She earned a bachelor's degree in business from the University of South Florida in Tampa and works by 2015 worked as a business analyst for the Florida Department of Revenue. As a young girl, she heard her mother and other family talking about her father, a professional football player. But her father's identity remained unknown to her.

At around four, a great-uncle and great-aunt adopted her and Trae grew up in Florida. She had love, discipline, and guidance to prepare her for adulthood, she said. Much like what Bobby's grandmother gave him.

"My mom was unable to take care of me back then," she said.

She completed high school not knowing the identity of her father. Some family members continued to make references to the fact her father could be Bobby Jackson, the ex-professional football player from Albany. In her late twenties she began to look at pictures of Bobby on the Internet and noticed the physical similarities of the two.

A few years ago, not long before Bobby's return to Albany for the ceremony retiring his number, Trae's aunt, Sandy Cofield contacted Bobby, telling him he likely had a daughter he had never met, he said.

While attending FSU, Bobby dated Sandy Cofield. During that period he slept once with her sister, Ann, and that resulted in the birth of Trae. At the time Ann was a student at Florida A & M University in Tallahassee.

During the same period Bobby flunked a geography course and believed he was ineligible to play football his senior year, he said. He left school and returned to Albany but before doing so Ann told him she was pregnant with his child.

"I didn't believe it then," he said. "I knew I wasn't the only guy she had been with." He left Tallahassee thinking his football career at FSU had ended and "trying not to think about" the possibility that he had fathered a child with Ann Cofield.

Later, in Albany, he received a telephone call from one of the Seminole coaches telling him he was eligible to play his senior year despite flunking the geography course. He had passed the other classes he was enrolled in.

Over the years Sandy Cofield called him a few times to tell him her sister's baby looked a lot like Bobby. But he made no effort to contact the child's mother or the child.

"For a long time I just didn't want to believe it was my child," he said.

Finally in 2013, Sandy convinced Bobby to contact Trae and gave him her phone number. On August 31 of that year, Bobby called Trae in Tallahassee, a few weeks before the ceremony to retire his number. He invited her to the event in Albany at the stadium. For the first time in her life, during that telephone conversation, she heard her father's voice.

She agreed to meet him in Albany. She traveled alone, making the two-hour drive from Tallahassee and thinking about what they might say to one another about a relationship that they had never had, she said. She arrived late for the ceremony honoring her father, but when they met Bobby hugged her. They talked and watched the game together.

"I was nervous," Trae said. "I didn't know what to expect, but after a while things flowed pretty naturally" as the two sat next to one another in the stadium.

Bobby introduced her to his mother, family members, and friends who came to support him that night. After the game he invited Trae to Uncle Willie Odom's house in Albany. There they talked more about their lives. Bobby told Trae about his relationship with her mother, brief as it was, in the 1970s, he said.

She shared with him stories of growing up, and the fact that her mother had been unable to raise her. But she was fortunate to have other family members who did so. She told him there were several times in her life when she felt hurt because she didn't know her father. She longed to know the identity of her father and wished for a loving relationship with him, Trae said.

Over the years, as Bobby's name came up within her family, and as Trae got older, she thought about contacting him, but was hesitant and "never tried to reach out to him," she said.

That night Bobby asked questions about Trae's life, her husband and her three children, his grandchildren. When Trae was a young girl she could run faster than most girls her age, she said. At one point she was the fastest girl in her school but never had the interest to pursue organized athletics. Of her three sons she has one in middle school who has exceptional speed on the football field, and she referred to him as a "natural-born leader."

A few weeks after Bobby and Trae met for the first time in Albany, he traveled to Tallahassee to attend an FSU football game, and he visited Trae, met his grandchildren, and his son-in-law.

After spending time with her family in Tallahassee, Bobby realized she was not only a "very beautiful" woman, but one with a loving family, he said.

"She got an education and accomplished her goals," Bobby said. "I was happy she had people in her life that cared about her. At the same time I regret I wasn't part of her life, but I was happy she was open to having a relationship with me."

Since the fall of 2013 the two, father and daughter, have stayed in contact through regular telephone conversations.

"I have no resentment toward him," Trae said. "I know he and my mother were both so young when she got pregnant. But I do wish I could've known earlier that he was my father. Since we met, he's been a pleasure to get to know."

No DNA test has been done to confirm that Bobby is Trae's father. Bobby had considered the possibility of the testing over the years, but all of that changed the night he met Trae in Albany, he said. They both agreed DNA testing would not be necessary.

"I'm convinced he is my father," she said.

"When I met her that night," Bobby said, "and looked at her, I knew she was my daughter. There was no need for any DNA test."

CHAPTER 17

In April 2015 a federal judge in the United States District Court for the Eastern District of Pennsylvania ruled in a lawsuit in favor of about 5,000 former NFL players, including Bobby Jackson. The judge agreed with the players that the league concealed the chronic cumulative effects of concussions.

The suit also charged that NFL teams routinely removed players from games in which they suffered concussions, and then returned the same players into the same games. News reports following Judge Anita Brody's 132-page ruling indicated that the NFL could award the plaintiffs collectively up to $900 million over the next several years.

On April 22, 2015, *The New York Times* reported that the landmark deal was originally reached in August 2013, but Judge Brody twice asked the two sides to revise their agreement, first to uncap the total amount of damages that could be paid for the conditions covered, and then to remove the limit on how much could be spent on medical monitoring.

The suit was filed on behalf of the players by the legal firm Zimmerman Reed, which has offices in Minneapolis, Minnesota and Scottsdale, Arizona. Specifically, the law firm was appointed to the Plaintiff's Steering Committee in the NFL Players' Concussion Injury Litigation. And the suit represented players who suffered head injuries and have symptoms associated with these injuries, and players who are not yet experiencing symptoms but want to be monitored.

The NFL made no admission of fault or guilt in connection with the financial settlement, the national news media reported.

Recent medical studies, according to the players' lawsuit, confirmed that retired NFL players face a substantially higher risk of Alzheimer's disease, dementia, and other neurological and memory-related disorders. Memory loss and symptoms of dementia may be linked to repeated concussions former NFL players suffered.

The suit argued, with the backing of documented medical research, that former players were clearly impaired when compared to similarly aged non-athletes. And there were significant differences with chronic brain trauma patterns in professional football players as opposed to men of comparable age who did not play football.

Maximum individual payouts from the lawsuit could range from one and a half million to five million dollars. For instance, an ex-player who is diagnosed with Alzheimer's or Parkinson's disease could receive up to $3.5 million. The average award to players could be approximately $190,000. The judge's ruling applies to all players who retired on or before July 7, 2014. After the verdict was released in April 2015, national news media quoted two lawyers who worked on behalf of the players.

"Today these courageous men and their families have made history," Christopher Seeger and Sol Weiss said. "Despite the health situations retired players face today and that more will unfortunately face in the future, they can take comfort that this settlement's benefits will be available soon, and will last for decades."

Playing football in high school, at the collegiate level, and in the NFL can easily result in many concussions. Bobby's teammates, opponents, and coaches called him one of the hardest hitters on the field at all three levels of competition. He had to hit hard, he said later. He had to prove that at five-foot nine and 170 pounds, he could play big and hit big. At times, he put fear in the hearts of those he played against.

At Albany High School in the early 1970s players said, "I got my bell rung," when they received a hard hit by a teammate at practice or during a game. Several of those he played against went on to outstanding collegiate and even professional careers, such as William Andrews of Thomasville, who played fullback for the Atlanta Falcons.

One of Bobby's most vicious hits in the NFL, and there were many, came against Williams who out-weighed him by several pounds. Within the rules in the 1970s for high school players to hit helmet-to-helmet, when Bobby hit that way, it sounded like an explosion. That kind of hitting from Bobby continued at FSU and throughout his career with the Jets.

"I know I had concussions during my career," Bobby said. "Who knows how many? I know they started at Albany High."

Like many players, when Bobby was in the NFL he often played hurt, sometimes taking pills and getting injections to lessen the pain, making it possible for him to continue playing. "I took lots of pills and got lots of shots," Bobby said. "That was what you had to do to keep playing."

The fifteen years of organized football, nine in the NFL, have caused him daily pain in his joints. Sometimes he has problems sleeping because of the pain, his short-term memory is affected, and, he said, "I truly believe my attention span suffers" as a result of playing football.

He does not like to fly because it causes anxiety, which he partly attributes to the years of hard physical contact while playing football.

"I take pills for my anxiety today," he said. "It's just something I've had to do for a long time now."

Before Bobby retired from the NFL in 1986, he watched a documentary called *Disposable Heroes: The Other Side of Football*, which had recently been released. Hollywood actor Peter Coyote narrated the HBO film, and it had a profound impact on Bobby as it explicitly exposed the underbelly of professional football, and the physical toll it takes on players.

Coyote begins by saying Americans love the NFL and watching "highly-skilled and highly-paid" players, and the heroic way they play the game.

Then the film turns dark. The film reported that the average NFL career is four and a half years, and most players will be forced to leave the game because of serious injuries or being cut from a team's roster before they reach the age of twenty-six. At that time there were around sixteen hundred players in the NFL and seventy-four percent did not earn a college degree. Most will sustain injuries from playing that they will suffer with the rest of their lives, the film reported.

Parts of the film include scenes from NFL games during the early 1980s that illustrate the often-violent hits, the way Bobby played, that marked that period. Any player during any season, the film reported, has an 80 percent chance of being injured, and when that happens they are confronted with two choices: not to play and sit on the bench, or take pain killers and play with the chance of worsening the injury.

"It's a no-win situation," Coyote said. One former player in the film called NFL players "replaceable parts," and the NCAA every year produced new parts.

Disposable Heroes profiled a few NFL players and the physical struggles they were experiencing after they retired from football. Jim Otto played center for the Oakland Raiders for fifteen years and has been inducted into the NFL Hall of Fame.

"When you talk professional football you don't talk job security," Otto said in the documentary. Players referred to Otto as "Iron Man" because of his longevity. He retired from the league in 1974. The Iron Man often "pays for it later," John Madden, Otto's former coach for the Raiders, said.

Otto's medical problems as a result of football did not end with the release of *Disposable Heroes*. In 2012, Otto gave an interview in which he said he has had 74 surgeries, including having his right leg amputated, as a result of football injuries. Otto also played football at the University of Miami in Florida.

"Watching that film back then," Bobby said, "just confirmed what I already knew. Everyone in the league is replaceable. But for the first time it made me think about my future and my health. That film had a big impact on me. Yeah, I was aware of a lot of what was in the film, but it just put things in perspective for me."

According to the NFL Players Association, the average career today is a little over three years. Players leave the league because of serious injury, retirement or being cut by a team. The shortest careers among players tend to be those who hit and get hit the most. For running backs it's about 2.57 years, wide receivers play on average 2.81 years, and cornerbacks 2.94 years.

Bobby's career defied the numbers. He started at cornerback for the Jets his rookie season in 1978 and held that position for the same team until 1985. That kind of tenure at that position is rare and indicates his toughness and durability.

Kickers and punters today have the longest careers in the NFL with an average of 4.87 years, followed by quarterbacks at about 4.4 years, according to the NFL Players Association.

Bobby said he is in better shape today physically than many others he played against and with, including his friend and former Jets' teammate wide receiver Wesley Walker, who has had a series of health problems much more serious than what Bobby has endured. Things once simple are more difficult for him now.

"Reading is harder now and sometimes I get stuck," Bobby said. "It takes me a while to understand what I read." It's not uncommon for Bobby to take several minutes to complete a short, uncomplicated passage. "It can be very frustrating."

Bobby maintains regular exercise and remains slender and in seemingly good physical shape. Part of his workout includes the Brazilian martial art known as jiu-jitsu. Sometimes during class he loses his balance during the simplest routines, gets light headaches, and sweats profusely when the others in class do not. He has had no major surgeries since his retirement as a result of injuries he sustained as a player.

Wesley Walker is just one of many players from Bobby's era who struggle with serious health issues related to football injuries. Some have died because of the injuries. In 1981 while playing the New England Patriots, Bobby broke his arm following a collision with running back Mosi Tatupu, who played in the NFL for fourteen seasons.

Mosi died of a heart attack in 2010 at age 54. In January 2015 *The Boston Globe* reported that his family learned five years after his death that he suffered from chronic traumatic encephalopathy or CTE, a disease that silently destroys the minds of athletes after repetitive blows to the head. Researchers at the Boston University of School of Medicine found the disease in the brains of 140 deceased athletes, many of them former football players like Mosi Tatupu.

Over the past several years, researchers have also documented and the national media has reported the higher than normal rate of suicide among former and current NFL players, as opposed to the general population, with some referring to the numbers as an epidemic.

Around the same time *The Boston Globe* reported new information about Mosi Tatupu and the condition of his brain when he died, Wesley Walker gave an interview to the *New York Daily News* expressing regret for playing thirteen seasons in the NFL.

Fame and money and athletic achievement from his NFL career were not worth the physical beating his body endured, Wesley said. Every day he's "in pain head to toe." Since his retirement in 1989 after thirteen seasons, the two-time Pro Bowler has had surgery on both shoulders, back surgery that required ten screws and a plate, spinal fusion surgery that required fourteen screws, and surgery for a torn Achilles.

Given the chance to do it all over again, he would've done it differently. "I would have taken another path," he said. "Maybe become a commentator. Just from a physical standpoint, there is no way I would put my body through what I do now. I don't wish this on anyone."

In the newspaper story Wesley, then 59 years old, referred to Chris Borland, who in March 2015 announced his retirement from the NFL because of his concerns about brain damage as a result of a long career. Borland, 24, played linebacker for the San Francisco 49ers in 2014 and became one of the top rookies in the league. He played at the University of Wisconsin and would've earned around $540,000 for the upcoming 2015 season.

Wesley said he wished he had done what Borland did. "You have to self-evaluate and know what your priorities are and what the situation is," he said. "I admire a guy who is going to look long-term and figure he's going to do something else and create another path. I would like to think people are getting smarter with that."

Wesley said doctors never diagnosed him with a concussion when he played for the Jets but is certain he sustained a few. Like what Bobby experienced the times he suffered injuries, Wesley said he experienced pressure from teammates, coaches, and even some trainers telling him if he could only play 50 percent of his capability, that's still better than 100 percent of his backup.

"Wesley and I have been close ever since we played together," Bobby said. "We still see a lot of one another doing appearances for the Jets. He's had it so much tougher than me. I've been more fortunate so far." But Bobby is worried about his declining health. "What will it be like if I can't get up and move? How will I handle that?"

Still, there is respect and appreciation for football, the game in which he has accomplished so much since he developed a passion for it at Albany High School. And there are no regrets, so far, such as those Wesley Walker expressed.

Bobby, from his boyhood days in Albany, went on to far surpass his junior high coaches' prediction. They said he was too small to play football. He is not resentful of the NFL for his physical challenges today, caused by years in the league, he said.

"Football is football, and it's a violent game," he said. "The league doesn't need to change a lot of rules just to try to make it safer. They need to do a better job of helping players after their careers end."

Bobby does not advocate major changes in the NFL, "a league making billions of dollars off us," to reduce the violence and injuries connected with it, he said. Players have to be willing to accept the risk.

It's "the love of money" that drives the league, and it needs to pay more attention to the "human value" of players, and how better to help them when they are in the league and when they retire, he said. Unlike when he played, some teams now provide financial counseling and help players earn their college degrees, as many come into the league without one, he said.

"There's more help out there now than when I played," he said, but more needs to be done to help players adjust during retirement. The financial awards from the suit are a beginning. "I don't know how much money I'll get from the lawsuit," he said. "There are a lot of players out there worse off than me."

EPILOGUE

I told Bobby's high school football coach, Ferrell Henry, that Bobby had been a participant in the Sun Dance, the sacred ritual of the Lakota, for four consecutive years. And I explained to Henry both the physical and mental sacrifices required to endure that religious ceremony, and that Bobby had completed his commitment to the Lakota.

"I'm not surprised," Henry said. "Bobby Jackson will do anything he sets out to do. If you told me he was going to be an astronaut, I wouldn't be surprised."

Growing up in poor neighborhoods and in the housing projects of Albany, in the 1960s and early '70s, Bobby made his mark by racing the garbage trucks, and later racing any boy who wanted to. Eventually beating them all.

He raced and played football with a big heart, but a heart often longing for his mother, who had moved away from Bobby and Albany when he was young.

His grandmother, Rebecca Jackson, cared for him for several years before he graduated from high school and left Albany on a football scholarship to FSU. She provided love, discipline, and encouragement.

Years passed, and Bobby did not know the whereabouts of his mother, Donna Mae Meeks. His father, Robert Charles Jackson, Sr., remained a vital part of Bobby's life until his death in 2004. Bobby admired his father, the man he wanted to be like.

Bobby reunited with his mother by happenstance in a Long Island courthouse not long after the Jets drafted him in 1978. And since that day mother and son have remained close.

He holds no grudges toward her for the years she chose to be away from him.

Bobby's early family life became complicated and painful when his young mother became pregnant by another man when his father was overseas serving in the military. It split his family apart and the pain, in some ways, has been long standing.

Bobby's own personal life, seven children by four different women and three born out of wedlock, has often led to complications and pain for the women he loved, and the children he fathered. In the case of one of his children, Trae Leonard born in 1977, Bobby didn't learn he was her father until their emotional meeting in 2013.

As Bobby struggled with drug addiction beginning around 2006, he managed to conceal it for the most part from his children. In 2009 he began to cleanse himself of the drugs. In 2014 he married Jacqueline Brown, a Lakota raised partly at Standing Rock Reservation in South Dakota.

"She has always been the woman for me," he said. "I'm fortunate to have her in my life."

Unimpressed by Bobby's NFL career, Jackie fell in love with him for other reasons when they met in the early 1980s. Bobby had liked that about her. And much more.

He had an outstanding eight-year career with the Jets at cornerback, becoming a tenacious hitter and leader on defense. He's forthright in his view that he was often overlooked because the Jets were not one of the top teams in the league during his tenure. Not being chosen to play in a Pro Bowl game, still hurts today, he said.

Jets All-Pro wide receiver Wesley Walker said Bobby was just as good, if not better, than All-Pro cornerback Lester Hayes of the Oakland Raiders. Bobby and Wesley made each other better at practice. Both ended up being two of the best in the league at their respective positions.

"He was the best I ever faced and that's the truth," Wesley said.

As a little boy, Bobby always had to prove himself to others because of his lack of size. He had to run faster and hit harder on the sandlot football fields of Albany. Same in high school, college, and in the NFL.

Since his retirement from the NFL, the Jets have remained a constant in his life. "The organization was good to me," Bobby said. "I've tried to give back some over the years." His face for the past few decades has been a familiar one in representing the Jets.

For instance, on May 20, 2015, he was one of seven people from the Jets representing the team along the Hudson River during Fleet Week. Bobby rode the US Coast Guard cutter, *Spencer,* during the parade of ships honoring the work of the military. Fleet Week brings together about eighteen hundred members of the Navy, Marines, and Coast Guard for activities in and around Manhattan that continue through Memorial Day.

On that day, the parade passed by Fort Hamilton in Brooklyn with a gun salute, and then came the solemn rendering of honors as the fleet passed the World Trade Center site.

"Just being a part of it, being around the military personnel and being out there in the harbor around Manhattan, it was a great experience," Bobby said. "I've always supported the military. There's a lot of military involvement in my family. It just put it all in perspective."

Bobby worked his way out of the poverty of his youth in Georgia through football. He worked harder still to excel at FSU and again for the Jets. Later, he made a mess of his life for a few years through crack cocaine, endangering himself and causing those who loved him to suffer. He lied regularly while a drug addict. But he worked to restore his life and to heal the wounds he had created.

By the summer of 2009, his first trip to the Sitting Bull Sun Dance Camp on Standing Rock Reservation in South Dakota, Bobby found something that gave him, and continues to give him today, spiritual strength, he said. He endured the physical and mental challenges of the demanding Sun Dance for four consecutive summers, beginning in 2010. The experience of that deepened his sense of his own childhood, the man that he became, and how he wants to live the rest of his life.

"I want to be a willing receptacle for the truth," Bobby said. "That's where I am now. At some point you have to put away childish things. I want to do the right thing with the rest of my time on earth. I'm dying in the truth."

As the sun rises over the prairie, let the dancing begin.

One of Bobby's early childhood homes at 713 "B" Corn Avenue in Albany, Georgia.

During his teenage years, Bobby lived at 671 Society Avenue with his grandmother, Rebecca Jackson. They were part of the public housing complex known as CME – Crime, Murder, and Execution. From Bobby's house he could see Albany High's football stadium where he dazzled fans with his speed and supreme athleticism.

Bobby's father, Robert Jackson, Sr. Bobby admired his father and aspired to be "like him." The photo was taken in the late 1950s or early '60s.

This is the Albany High coaching staff from the early 1970s. Back row left to right: Ronnie Archer, Jack Hitson, Darrell Willett, Johnny Young, Willie Magwood and Phil Spooner. Kneeling is Head Coach Ferrell Henry, who Bobby considered a "father figure" and helped him secure a scholarship at FSU in 1974.

His final and best year at FSU, 1977. And the second season there for Head Coach Bobby Bowden. The team finished 10-2 overall, ranked 14th in the nation, and defeated Texas Tech 40-17 in the Tangerine Bowl.

Bobby's sophomore year, 1975, at FSU. He started at cornerback all four years and became part of one of the best defensive backfields in Seminole history.

Bobby broke up a long pass during a game in the early 1980s intended for Miami Dolphin tight end, number 80, Joe Rose. Bobby's teammates are number 28 Darrol Ray and number 37 Tim Moreso.

Bobby prepares to defend against wide receiver Cedric Jones during a game with the New England Patriots.

This was taken in the locker room in Miami after the Jets lost to the Dolphins in the 1982 AFC playoff game. Bobby's son, Robert Thomas, is with him.

Bobby suffered a neck injury during a game with the New England Patriots in the early '80s. This and other injuries would shorten his NFL career.

Left to right is Bobby and teammates Mark Gastineau and Wesley Walker taken at Hofstra University, the site of Jets' preseason camp.

This promotional photo was taken after Bobby's career ended in 1986. He played for the Atlanta Falcons that year.

Brothers David and Bobby Jackson kneeling over Bobby's FSU Football Hall of Fame marker in Tallahassee. Bobby was inducted in the early 1990s. David died in 2017.

Bobby Butler and Bobby Jackson, two of the greatest cornerbacks to play at FSU. They returned to Tallahassee a few years ago for an event to honor Coach Bobby Bowden. Both players had outstanding NFL careers.

This photo of Bobby's mother, Donna Mae Newsome and his uncle, Charlie B. Jackson was taken a few years ago in Albany. Donna Mae left Bobby when he was a boy and for more than a decade the two had no contact with each other.

This is on display at the FSU campus and is in recognition of Bobby being inducted into the school's Football Hall of Fame.

Left to right: Bobby, Uncle Charlie B. Jackson, Bobby's brother David, and his cousin, Charlie B. Jackson, Jr.

Taken in 2013 at Bobby's Long Island home, here are six of his seven children: Robert Thomas (standing), Chante', Asia (sitting on floor), Tenisha, Bobby, Indya, and Ashun.

Bobby's seventh child, Trae Leonard, was born in 1977. But the two did not meet until 2013 when Trae travelled from her Tallahassee home to see Bobby the night his high school football number was retired in Albany.

Bobby at Sun Dance in 2013 at Standing Rock Reservation. From left to right: Giordano, Gilberto Borzacchini, Bobby and Luciano.

Here Bobby's wife, Jackie, is dressed in the tradition of the Lakota. She grew up at Standing Rock and is a descendant of the great Lakota warrior and holy man, Sitting Bull.

Left to right: I'm with Bobby and James Harpe, and we were all teammates at Albany High in the early 1970s. This was taken in the summer of 2014 on Long Island as I began the research for this book.

Taken in 2016 and from left to right: Wesley Walker, Bobby, Shafer Suggs, and Maurice Tyler. All former teammates who were attending a Jets' alumni reunion.

The night Bobby's high school number was retired in Albany in 2013: Former teammates and family members from left to right; Johnny Coleman, Ernest Worthy, Pop Odom, Danny Jackson, Charlie Jackson and Bobby.

Bobby's retired Albany High jersey is being held by the school's athletic director, Archie Chatmon.

Taken the same night in 2013: Cousin Charlie Johnson and Bobby.

Bobby's brothers and sisters on his mother's side of the family and taken in the early 1970s: Back row, left to right; Sabrina, Jimmy and Adrian. Front row, left to right; Danny, Cynthia, Phyllis, Donna and Bobby.

Taken in Albany in 2016: Bobby's uncle Marvin Newsome and his mother, Donna Mae.

Bobby's last year in the NFL, 1986, was with the Atlanta Falcons. This photo hangs in the Albany Sports Hall of Fame where Bobby was inducted after his professional football career ended.

AUTHOR'S NOTE

I was honored to write this book about Bobby Jackson, who I first met and came to admire in the fall of 1972 as we were both part of Albany High School football team that year. I once wrote in an earlier book that Bobby played football like a "god," and the rest of us on that team were mere mortals.

The following year I played quarterback, with Bobby on the receiving end of some of my passes. With his great speed, leaping ability, and determination, he was an easy target. Following Bobby's career at FSU and for the Jets, I was proud of him, as were others from Albany who knew and respected him. Our hometown hero.

It's easy for me to remember Bobby's supreme athleticism on the field and just as easy to remember that he was a decent, humble guy in high school. Never boastful, as others might be who excelled the same way he did.

When Bobby asked me a few years ago if I'd be interested in writing his story, my response was an immediate "yes." I was excited then and remained that way throughout the project.

We spent many hours talking about his life when I began interviewing Bobby in the summer of 2014 at his home on Long Island. These interviews continued by telephone and when Bobby came to Albany to visit during that period.

I was able to interview family members, former teammates and coaches, and even some of his opponents in the NFL. Thanks to all who shared their stories and contributed to the making of this book.

I also referred to several internet sources and newspaper accounts from Bobby's playing days to help with the story.

Writing Bobby's story obviously allowed me to learn much more about him than I knew when we were in high school together. To know his past in detail, the struggles he encountered and overcame, has given me even greater respect for what he has accomplished.

Finally, thank you to my editor, Rosemary Barnes, of Atlanta for all your hard work on this manuscript.

I hope all who read this book will be inspired by Bobby Jackson's life.

ABOUT THE AUTHOR

Bill Lightle lives in Fayetteville, Georgia, with his wife, Phyllis. He is the author of several non-fiction books and the John Maynard and Abby Sinclair novels.

After the publication of his first book, *Made or Broken: Football & Survival in the Georgia Woods,* the Georgia State Senate passed a resolution stating, "Bill Lightle has demonstrated his passion for education, history, and the furtherance of social justice…it is fitting and proper that the outstanding accomplishments of this remarkable and distinguished Georgian be recognized."

www.billlightle.com

Lightle's books are available through Amazon.

Made in the USA
Columbia, SC
22 July 2024

38531542R00133